MICK THOMAS
THESE ARE THE DAYS
-STORIES AND SONGS-

MELBOURNE BOOKS

Published by Melbourne Books
Level 9, 100 Collins Street,
Melbourne, VIC 3000
Australia
www.melbournebooks.com.au
info@melbournebooks.com.au

Copyright © Mick Thomas 2017

All rights reserved. No part of this publication may be reproduced, stored in a retrieval system, or transmitted in any form or any means electronic, mechanical, photocopying, recording or otherwise without the prior permission of the publishers.

Every effort has been made to identify the copyright holders of all images included in this publication. Any person who believes they have not been properly attributed may contact the publisher for correction in any future printing.

All text by Mick Thomas unless otherwise credited. All songs M. Thomas, reprinted courtesy of Mushroom Music except Our Sunshine - M. Thomas (Mushroom Music) / P. Kelly (Sony/ATV), Peggy and Col M. Thomas/ M. Wallace (Control) TBA and Wide Open Road by D. McComb Mushroom Music. The lyrics to The Red Pirate of Boracay by Adam Gibson, Control. Photographs by Mark Hopper unless otherwise indicated and most of the posters by Jen Huntley.

National Library of Australia
Cataloguing-in-Publication entry
Author: Mick Thomas.
Title: These Are The Days: Stories and Songs.
ISBN: 9781925556056 (paperback)
Subjects: Thomas, Michael.
Musicians--Australia--Biography.
Guitarists--Australia--Biography.

Art Direction: Sean Hogan – Trampoline
Design: Sean Hogan and Ellen Yan Cheng – Melbourne Books
Cover Art: Jen Huntley

FOR SASKIA EDITH – I REALLY DO HOPE THIS HELPS MAKES SOME SENSE OF IT ALL TO YOU ONE DAY.

CONTENTS

Chapter	Pg	Stories and Songs
	06	Foreword *by Darren Hanlon*
	10	Introduction *by Mick Thomas*
01	14	The Lonely Goth & *Chord Chart*
02	22	You Remind Me & *Chord Chart*
03	28	Monday's Experts & *Chord Chart*
04	34	Gallipoli Rosemary & *Chord Chart*
05	40	Hard Currency & *Chord Chart*
06	46	Baked A Cake & *Chord Chart*
07	52	Sisters Of Mercy & *Chord Chart*
08	60	When You Go & *Chord Chart*
09	66	Shank's Pony & *Chord Chart*
10	72	Knockbacks In Halifax & *Chord Chart*
11	78	Our Sunshine & *Chord Chart*
12	84	Step In Step Out & *Chord Chart*
13	90	Anywhere But Here & *Chord Chart*
14	98	Wide Open Road & *Chord Chart*
15	104	Forgot She Was Beautiful & *Chord Chart*
16	110	The Ballad Of Peggy And Col & *Chord Chart*

CONTENTS

Chapter	Pg	Stories and Songs
17	118	Maltby By-pass & *Chord Chart*
18	124	A Tale They Won't Believe & *Chord Chart*
19	130	Father's Day & *Chord Chart*
20	136	Selling The Cool Car For You & *Chord Chart*
21	142	Can I Sleep On Your Floor? & *Chord Chart*
22	148	The Red Pirate Of Boracay & *Chord Chart*
23	154	Scorn Of The Women & *Chord Chart*
24	160	All The Roads & *Chord Chart*
25	166	The Rain In My Heart & *Chord Chart*
26	172	The Last Of The Tourists & *Chord Chart*
27	180	Tommy Didn't Want You & *Chord Chart*
28	188	The Cap Me Granda' Wore & *Chord Chart*
29	194	Away Away & *Chord Chart*
30	200	Australian Flag Bikini & *Chord Chart*
31	206	For A Short Time & *Chord Chart*
	218	The Albums
	220	Acknowledgements
	222	The Author

FOREWORD

In the industrial port town of Bunbury on the West Australian coast, Mick Thomas grits his teeth and looks out past the microphone into a thin crowd of drunk revellers, rowdy in their little groups, eager to yell for either of  the two songs they've come to hear. Before the show I'd wished him luck; his reserve tank seemed low and it did look a bit rough. After a long and gruelling transcontinental tour of many highs, it seems anticlimactic to end this way. I am just his young lead guitarist and yet to learn that any Australian touring musician in their right mind has vowed more than once to never return to Bunbury, and then wonder what twist of fate has brought them back.

Foreword

Mick opts to start the set alone so I'm afforded the rare opportunity to sit out front and take it all in. He starts with a deep cut, The Wind and the Rain. A tender reading at that. He puts down the guitar, and holstering the mandolin starts speaking a story in a more hushed way than was his usual roistering bantering tone, almost like we are all sitting across a kitchen table from him. It's a story about a husband and wife working different shifts, never sharing the marital bed at the same time. One morning after a long night the man decides in a pique of tenderness to sleep on the side of his beloved, if only to be closer to her, but when he finds that side cold and unwrinkled by sleep, suspects infidelity and huffily rolls over to his own side only to find the warmth there, his wife having had the same thought. Mick starts gently strumming the opening chords to his ballad Step In, Step Out on the mandolin.

I am touched by the story, not to mention intrigued by this little flash of illumination, a clue to a song I've enjoyed for a long time. Mick continues like this for a few more songs, giving humble introductions. I look around at the crowd and hope they know they're getting what I think is shaping up to be the best show of the tour, a performance both candid and improvised. All the more powerful in it's restraint. Mick Thomas is renowned as a generous performer but this has nothing to do with show business. I'm in the process of learning yet another lesson, that situations of defeating adversity can bring out the best in certain artists. I guess it's something to do with the break in pressure of usual high profile settings, mixed with feelings of sweet melancholy and despairing at the injustice of it all. Whatever the cocktail of emotions flowing through the neural pathways of Mick Thomas this night he laid out a set both revealing and vivid.

I witnessed that then just as I write this now, as a fan. I've been so since a high school classmate returned from seeing U2 in Brisbane and raved more about the support band and how the lead singer looked like a bushranger from where he sat up in the nosebleeds. During one epic song about murderous cannibals he wielded his guitar in the air like an axe. This particular classmate had already achieved the formidable feat of taste-making me into appreciating the finer songwriting nuances of the Cold Chisel catalogue, so I therefore trusted him and accepted the loan of the Weddings Parties Anything double album cassette.

And thus Mick Thomas took a seat at the round table of the other songwriting heroes of my adolescence. I wore off that tape's high frequencies from frequent listens in Dad's HR while we took trips or drove around town, grizzled when we had to eject for the 4GY news, stretched out the folded lyric sheet like an accordion to study the words and try to work out the stories behind the songs.

Preceding page left: Taken at Darren Hanlon's short-lived series of Monday night gigs called 'Fraser Island' in Brunswick. Melbourne, 2011. Photo: Mark Hopper

Preceding page right: Greendale Hotel, 2014. Photo: Mark Hopper

Desperately wishing to be able to write meaningful songs myself, I started listening to the music I loved like a mechanical engineer. What made this song special? Why was this particular word used instead of another? Which Henry Lawson poems inspired Roaring Days? Who's heart is being rained in? I now know enough to fight the impulse to take songs apart completely to study the pieces lest when they are reassembled they look wonky. But just the right amount of information could make them shine even brighter.

At seventeen it was still a farfetched notion that I might soon leave my town and see a Weddings Parties Anything show for myself, let alone join a band who'd eventually support them. From where I sit now at the other end of this story it all seems pretty natural how Mick Thomas and I met and became mates and have since played and toured, wrote and recorded together. But in the mix of it all the seventeen year old nerd in me has snuck out of the bag a few times and battered Mick with questions.

'Where did you write Fathers Day?' I asked him.
'Upstairs at the at Annandale Hotel,' he said, 'Room 5.'
'Ya kidding?' I was working there at the time, 'You were living at the Annandale?'
'Yup.'

My next shift when I got back from tour, I grabbed the keys and went and had a look. It was being used for storage. Stacks of paint tins, broken chairs, a can of flyspray. A single bed still lay underneath it all. Maybe this was his old one?

And so with this book Mick Thomas has opened a door slightly ajar, and what lies behind are old musty rooms like that one, as well as long hot car journeys, photographs stuck in pages of books, meals eaten, jokes told, friends found and lost again. The clay of the life of Mick Thomas from which he's moulded his life's work.

In the bandroom of the venue in Bunbury we quickly pack up our gear so we can escape the place before it transforms into a full blown night club. Mick clips up the case of his old coin-battered Maton, the very one a lot of his songs have flowed out of.

'I was just paraphrasing Italo Calvino,' he says of the Step In, Step Out preamble, 'It's from a short story he wrote in a book called Difficult Loves'

Well this has opened a can of worms, but I should save the rest of my questions for the drive. A loud electronic pulse has started up just beyond our door. We push through the throng of young local party goers and out to the van for the long journey back to Perth.

❧

Darren Hanlon
November 2016

It'd been a tough week, coming towards the end of a generally tough time.

Our first born child had just clocked up her eighty-fifth day in hospital, and despite the doctor's assurance that she wouldn't be joining the one hundred day club, there seemed a fair chance this dubious honour was coming our way. On the home front we were just hanging in there, doing enough to keep things ticking over and spending most of our time in transit to the NICU of the hospital out at Heidelberg.

Introduction

The two dogs that had ruled our lives for so long couldn't fathom what was happening; why the walks weren't forthcoming and dinner was always late, and why the house was so generally troubled. To make things much worse, the younger of the two, Finley, had been sick for some time with various cancers, and six months previously we'd agreed to have his front leg amputated. Some dogs adapt well to this, but our little bloke just wasn't one of them. It was painfully obvious his fourteen years on this earth were coming to an end.

Disturbed by our generally distracted behaviour, he took to limping out to sleep in the bungalow studio out the back — something he'd never been permitted to do in the past. I was hopeful he'd hang on until our baby came home and that we could at least inhabit the same space for however long he could manage. I just would've loved a picture of them together, I suppose.

But it wasn't to be, and one awful cold July day the decision was made. It was quick enough, and handled well by people whose job it is to handle these things well, and there you had it. After fourteen tumultuous years our little fellow Finley was no more.

After it was all settled and done, we were faced with the reality: Jen had to get out to the hospital to be with the baby and I had to get to work at the pub. She said she'd drop me there as it was raining and then head out to Heidelberg. But as we drove into Clifton Hill, the traffic seemed to build and build. Getting across Alexandra Parade was going to take forever, and I suggested she drop me off and I take the tram or walk if the rain wasn't too heavy. So she pulled the van off the main drag into a side street, I got out and she drove away. I found myself standing next to an old bookshop with a mural painted on the wall. It's something I must have driven, walked and ridden by countless times, but as it goes on days like this, I stopped and looked at the mural painted there. It was a poem written by long-gone Melbourne poet Shelton Lea. This is how it reads:

Days

there are no old days
no good old days
no, they were the days days

these are the days
and more days
and all days.

Shelton Lea 1946–2005

It took me another twenty minutes to get down to the pub, and when I walked in I guess everyone could see I was upset. Somebody finally asked and I told them our poor little dog had died that day. Someone tried to console me and someone else commented that geez we were having a bad trot, and this made me think for a minute. Well, not even a minute. For an instant all the three previous months of turmoil and worry added up to that moment in front of the mural in Clifton Hill and all I could be sure of was that there was great stuff in front of us and this was a great time in itself. No, I replied, things were going great. And I was right.

And so the name of this book, *These Are the Days*, comes directly from that poem. I spend so much time artistically lugging around the weight of a back catalogue, in that the legacy of the fifteen years I spent with Weddings, Parties, Anything seems to be the only thing that concerns a lot of people. But as I write it's 2015, which means I've spent a longer period as an artist post-WPA than I did with the band as a functioning unit. This is not to take anything away from those years, those line-ups, records, shows and songs. It's just to say that I need to keep going, to keep hopping along on three legs if that's all that's available. And putting together a collection of songs and stories like this — including some of the old ones that still find their way into my life — alongside the newer titles is the best way I know to move on to the next thing.

In these pages I've tried to write introductions to the songs that have been with me through these last seventeen years and more, using them as jumping-off points in the lives of the people who have made this music. In a lot of people's minds it mightn't all be from the crucial or iconic period of my life artistically or personally, but believe me, enough has happened in this time, as I'm sure it will continue to do. And so, as the poem says, *these are the days*.

❧

Mick Thomas
Northcote, 2015

Preceding page: The wall, the poem. Clifton Hill, 2017. Photo: Mark Hopper

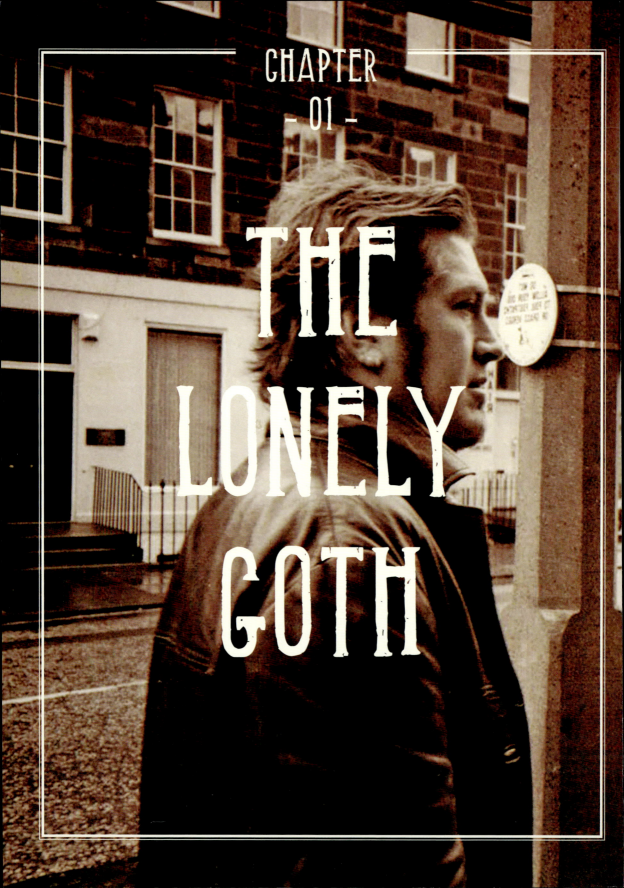

READ ENOUGH INTERVIEWS WITH SONGWRITERS AND IT'S INEVITABLE YOU'LL ENCOUNTER THE LINES 'OH THAT ONE JUST FELL OUT, I SCRIBBLED IT DOWN IN FIVE MINUTES AND THERE IT WAS IN ITS ENTIRETY'. MORE OFTEN THAN NOT THIS WILL BE IN REFERENCE TO THEIR BEST OR BIGGEST COMMERCIAL SONG AND I THINK IT'S DIFFICULT NOT TO BE CYNICAL AND CONCLUDE THIS CANDID EXPOSITION IS DESIGNED TO MAKE YOU FEEL IN AWE OF THEIR ARTISTIC PROWESS. ('FELL OUT' MAKES IT SOUND LIKE A GIRAFFE GIVING BIRTH DOESN'T IT?). BUT ACCEPTING THAT IT *DOES* HAPPEN (SONGS BEING WRITTEN QUICKLY I MEAN, AS WELL AS GIRAFFES GIVING BIRTH) AND THEY OCCASIONALLY DO 'JUST FALL OUT', MY FEELING IS IT'S MORE TO DO WITH THE SUBCONSCIOUS SHAPING OF AN IDEA OVER A PERIOD OF TIME THAN ANYTHING

Certainly, for me as a writer, these are the ones I suspect I've been grappling with internally for some time in a conceptual sense. In the back of your mind the tune may already be there somewhere, or perhaps some of the lines or rhymes, or at least the general theme of the song-to-be. I think a lot of the more difficult decisions have already been made by the time you actually pick up the guitar and open the Spirax notebook. And it's always decisions (or indecision) that will cost you time in any human endeavour.

And so it goes with 'The Lonely Goth'. The Bill Forsyth film *Local Hero* came out in 1983, and I have strong memories of the first few times I saw it. Firstly with some folksy types I was living with in Brunswick. They made some sort of hot whisky drink and sat me in front of the Sunday evening television premiere, and for a while Melbourne's inner north disappeared as the wilds of northern Scotland took hold of my consciousness. I bought the video and watched it regularly with friends at the house down by the creek in Northcote, where the Weddings had their home base throughout the eighties and early nineties.

The relevant thing about *Local Hero* is there's one solitary punk rock girl who seems a constant presence in the main street of the northern Scottish town where the film is set. I can't recall her being part of the actual film plot, more a silent witness to the goings-on of the film itself. She's sullen and despondent, but kind of endearing as well.

When I travelled around Scotland for the first time in the late eighties I couldn't get over just how accurate this observation was. That solitary example of disaffected youth seemed to be prevalent in almost every provincial centre.

And then years later, with the Weddings not long finished, I remember sitting in a coffee shop up in the Barossa en-route to Adelaide and seeing a haughty young chap come walking down the street in full gothic regalia. It was such a grand statement to be making on a daily basis — and one so potentially fraught with danger in a place like that. To me the situation had a direct correlation with *Local Hero*'s solitary punk rocker.

I think it's significant 'The Lonely Goth' was written (fell out) right at the end of 1999, probably on one of my first solo tours post-WPA. There is something in the loneliness of the subject matter and the rejection of the mainstream social path that resounded with where I was at the time emotionally. After fifteen years of being part of a really rowdy troupe, suddenly here I was, far from home, sitting and having a coffee on my own. It was liberating, relaxing and at the same time uncomfortably quiet.

I know when the artist Craig Smith illustrated the song for a children's story, that we made into a film clip, I was really happy with the weight he gave to the characters. Speaking to him recently, he commented that he might have been a little heavy-handed — that he made some of the antagonists too awful and ugly. But I'm happy with the grotesque element he brought to the tale. As much as I've chosen to make light of the main character, I really don't like a lot of the other people in the story. I suppose growing up in Australian country towns, my allegiances are totally with the Lonely Goth himself.

'The Lonely Goth' was certainly one of the pivotal songs in building a repertoire post-WPA, and one we all had really high hopes for. It was always destined to be one of the cornerstones of the first fully-fledged Sure Things studio album I would put together. The main line-up that would play on that album was short-lived — Darren Hanlon, Rosie Westbrook and Michael Barclay — which was unfortunate as it was pretty much exactly what I wanted the band to be, and what I wanted the record to sound like. Jerry Boys coming out from England to work on it seemed an adventurous thing to do (if not financially questionable for a totally independent production) and for a moment there, everything seemed to be heading in the right direction.

For a moment ...

Preceding page left: Newtown, Edinburgh, 1998

Preceding page right: From left: Darren Hanlon, Michael Barclay, Mick and Rosie Westbrook. Greendale, 2000. Photo: Mark Hopper

Opposite: An Illustration from The Lonely Goth Picture Book *by Craig Smith with kind permission*

M. THOMAS
THE LONELY GOTH
MUSHROOM MUSIC

(Riff)
D / / / | G / Em / | D / / / | G / Em / |

(Verse)
D / / / | G / Em / | D / / / | G / Em / |
Velvet pants and a big top hat it's a little hot to be dressed like that   Down near the

D / / / | G / Em / | C / / / | G / / / |
war memorial he's propped in a big black cape with twelve hole docs

D / / / | G / Em / | D / / / | G / Em / |
(he's wearing twelve hole docs)   Now he

D / / / | G / Em / | D / / / | G / Em / |
almost made his aunty faint when he stopped at the chemist for some black nail paint

D / / / | G / Em / | C / / / | G / / / |
He just stood there hand on hips he said 'Aunty Em it'll match my lips'.

(chorus)
A / / / | A / / / |
I heard his father and his mother say

F#m / / / | F#m / / / |
What possessed the boy to dress that way

G / (F#) / | Em / / / |
But don't you try and bring him down
C / / / | G / / / | D / / / | G / Em / | D / / / | G / Em / |
He's a lonely goth in a country town

(Verse)
Now his father's family settled here in another time it was a long gone year
He knows about them all you see they're buried at the local cemetery (rest in peace)
Now there's a girl in the next town that he knows they met at a Marilyn Manson show
They write letters and they swap spells they'll be together one day in hell

THE LONELY GOTH

(chorus)

(mid)

F#m / / / | F#m / / / | G / / / | G / / / |
To dress like that 'round here you'd guess that he likes being close to death

A / / / | A / / / | A / / / | A / / / |
He doesn't like footy he doesn't like cars but he didn't mind Coppolla's Dracula

(Verse)
Oneday he'll be rid of this place run like mascara down a pale white face
He doesn't believe in a god above but could you ever doubt his mother's love

(Chorus)
(extra chorus bits) - all over G / (F#) / | Em / / / | *progression*
And what will the blokes at the bottom (top) pub say
And the women down at here CWA
But it's eye of newt and tongue of bat
As he walks 'round town with his mum's black cat
And if you'd been through all he'd been through
Then you'd turn white and you'd frown too
He's the bravest boy behind the frown

C / / / | G / / / | D / / / | G / Em / |
Of a lonely goth in a country town   And he's

C / / / | G / / / | D / / / | G / Em / |
evoked the wrath of a country town   He's the

C / / / | G / / / | D / / / | G / Em / |
only one   for miles around   It's a mining

D / / / | G / Em / | D / / / | G / Em / |
town   a fishing town   a shearing

D / / / | G / Em / | D / / / | G / Em / |
town   a quiet little country town a quiet little country

D / / / | G / Em / | D / / / | G / Em / | D →
town

Take me home, lonesome road … Footscray, 1999

I WROTE THIS ONE WHILE STILL ON TOUR WITH THE WEDDINGS — IF NOT THE FINAL TOUR THEN WELL TOWARDS THE END. WE'D HAD A DATE TO FILL IN PERTH AND SO PHIL STEPHENS, WHO WAS PROMOTING THAT PART OF THE RUN, DECIDED TO PUT US INTO MOJOS FOR AN UNANNOUNCED SHOW. PETE LAWLER WAS THERE, AND SO WERE THE TIDDAS GIRLS. THE VENUE  WAS PACKED, AND WE'D MADE A RULE THAT NOBODY WAS TO PLAY ANY OF THEIR OWN ORIGINAL SONGS — IT WAS TO BE ALL COVERS.

It was a lot of fun. Pete brought the house down with a spirited version of 'Tainted Love', and as Sally Dastey from Tiddas had been playing with Pete and half of the Weddings for her solo side project, they had a good swag of songs to choose from. I can't remember what I sang. I recall Stephen O'Prey working his way through a pretty laboured version of the Irish folk standard 'Lannegan's Ball', with the club's head security guy on bodhran. It'd seemed a good idea when we suggested it, but it's a long tune and even though the guy was a fine upstanding Irishman he didn't quite have the rhythm Stephen was after. I fear it was a tough five minutes of his life.

After the show we dragged the party back to the hotel where we were staying in Perth, but somehow I didn't have the heart for it. Perhaps it was the end of the band looming in my mind, or it could have been a dozen other reasons, but the whole hotel room singalong thing can be hard to take if you aren't totally in the mood (and with a bunch of voices of that calibre the thing can become quite competitive — it requires real energy to take part).

The fact I wasn't keen was significant; in the early days of Weddings, Parties, Anything this had been one of the on-road activities I'd loved the most. I don't think anyone in the band around the late eighties could forget the marathon sessions we had — especially with Paul Kelly and the Coloured Girls/Messengers. There was actually talk (mainly from our side, I think) of doing an entire tour together and setting up the hotel rooms each night to get these things recorded, but nothing came of it. Producing anything of quality was much more technically unwieldy in those days, and I think it'd just seemed too hard to wrangle. Looking back I'd say it was probably a good thing, but I can't help wondering now how it might (or mightn't) have stood the test of time.

Anyway, deciding to leave Lawler and the Tiddas girls with the rest of the band, I saw fit to sneak off back to the room I was sharing with Stephen O'Prey, and ended up watching an old black and white film on the ABC. From memory it was called something like *I Was Happy There*, and it concerned an Irish girl's search for romantic fulfilment in London in the fifties, and it was kind of nice and soothing in a sweet, sad way. Somebody later told me it was an Ealing Picture, but I haven't been able to find anything about it at all. It's just one of those late-night ABC British films you might never lay eyes on again.

After a while Stephen came back to the room, and he was in a strangely subdued and reflective mood as well. So I guess it was the film, the approaching demise of the band, and the growing realisation that audiences seemed to be getting younger and younger that gave me the song.

Certainly, it's a tune that's served me well, another foundation tune more or less, for my repertoire post-WPA.

Recently, I was at the pub with Gus Agars, one of the rotating band of Roving Commission drummers. A young woman walked past and nodded in a familiar kind of way. I nodded back and smiled casually at Gus (who's about twenty years younger than me). He laughed and told me I still 'had it' after all these years. And then the woman came past again and nodded once more, this time more definitely. We basically went through the whole scenario again a few more times, until she finally said hello and asked if I was actually Mick Thomas from Weddings, Parties, Anything, to which I replied that I was.

Then the young woman said she had something to show me. So she started undoing the shirt she was wearing, which seemed provocative enough in a crowded bar. What she wanted us to see was that underneath the shirt was an old WPA t-shirt. While I gloated, she explained that it was her mother's and she'd borrowed it as hers were all in the wash, and did I want to speak to her mother on the phone? And I suppose when life imitates art in this fashion you really just have to laugh sometimes. Well, don't you?

'You Remind Me' is another of the tracks produced and engineered by Jerry Boys, assisted by Siiri Metsar for the *Dust on My Shoes* album. Interestingly enough, that's Mark 'Squeezebox' Wally guesting on the accordion.

Preceding page left: WPA at Fitzroy Football Ground. Melbourne, 1998. From left: 'Squeezebox' Wally, Michael Barclay, Jen Anderson, Paul Thomas, Mick and Stephen O'Prey

Preceding page right and opposite: Mick, Tiddas (Lou, Ami, Sal) and Rosy Westbrook. Dandenong Ranges Folk Festival, 2000. Photo: Mark Hopper

M. THOMAS

YOU REMIND ME

MUSHROOM MUSIC

(capo 5th fret)

(Riff)
Am / G / | Am / E7 / | x4

(Verse)
Am / / / | E7 / / / | F / / / | D7 / / / |
Maybe it's the way her hair hung down across the collar of her dress

Am / / / | E7 / / / | F / / / | G7 / / / |
Maybe it's the way she was   laughing with her friends

Am / / / | E7 / / / | F / / / | D7 / / / |
She was too young and I could see a thing with which I shouldn't really mess

Am / / / | E7 / / / | F / / / | G / / / | F / / / |G/ / / |
But when I'd finished playing   I was glad she'd stayed until the end

Am / / / | G / / / |
(then I said to my friend)

(chorus)
F / / / | G / / / | C / (b) / | Am / / / |
She reminds me of someone that I used to know

F / / / | G / / / | Am / (b) / | C / G / |
She reminds   me of   someone I knew long ago

Am / (b) / | C / E7 / |
Someone that I used to know

(verse)
The band were laughing at the way I quickly packed up all my stuff
Somebody said I was rising for a fall
But when she laughed at nearly every word I said it was enough
Her friends were laughing too I got the biggest laugh of all (when I said)

(chorus)
You know you remind me of someone that I used to know
You remind me of someone I knew long ago
Someone that I used to know

F / / / | F / / / | G / / / | G / / / |
I couldn't put my finger on it

E7 / / / | E7 / / / | F / / / | F / / / |
Thought I'd give anything to know

F / / / | F / / / | G / / / | G / / / |
She strung me along for near an hour

E7 / / / | E7 / / / | E7 / / / | E7 / / / |
And then she said she had to go oh and by the way Her mother

F / / / | F / / / | G / / / | G / / / |
said to say hello   (ahhh no)   Her mother

F / / / | F / / / | G / / / | G / / / |
said to say hello   hello   hello

(verse)
And in an instant twenty years just turned to dust
And I thought about one summer and a squalid room I'd shared
With a girl who just left university but knew it all
Well she left me for some other life but I'm still standing here
And it's surprising what you can see when the lights are focused right
All of the demons and the ghosts you might have met along the way
I told her to tell her mum that we should catch up one night
But really I was happy we were flying out next day
(After all to a girl like that what could I say)

(chorus)
You know you remind me of someone that I used to know
You remind me of someone I knew long ago
Someone that I used to know

F / / / | G / / / | Am / / / | G →

F / / / | G / / / | C / (b) / | Am / / / |
(Next day) Beef or chicken?   The hostess asked me on the plane

F / / / | G / / / | C / (b) / | Am / / / |
I could not answer something had stalled inside my brain

F / / / | G / / / | C / (b) / | Am / / / |
Are you all right sir? She asked She touched me on the head.

F / / / | G / / / | C / (b) / | Am / G / | E7 / / / | E7 -
She smiled at me a little bit and this is what she said

(chorus)
(She said) you remind me of someone that I used to know
You remind me ahhh come on how did your song go?
You remind me of someone I knew long ago
Someone that I used to know
Someone I knew long ago
Someone that I used to know

CHAPTER
— 03 —

MONDAY'S EXPERTS

IT'S A FUNNY THING HOW A SMALL SONG CAN CAUSE SO MUCH STRIFE. HOW A WELL-INTENTIONED, REASONABLY INNOCUOUS COMMENT ON MODERN LIFE CAN BECOME THE FOCUS OF SO MUCH EXTERNAL PRESSURE THAT YOU FEEL LIKE TOTALLY WALKING AWAY FROM IT.

HERE'S HOW IT ALL PANNED OUT FOR THIS HELPLESS, INOFFENSIVE DITTY.

After the success of Father's Day — the heavy rotation airplay, chart success and Aria Award for Song of the Year — RooArt Records decided time was ripe to put all our efforts into a new album and single. We promptly recorded a bunch of songs in Melbourne, and then they packed Pete Lawler and myself off to the UK to mix them. We came back with the album *King Tide* ready to go, and after the usual arguments and industry research (playing it to your mates) it was decided 'Monday's Experts' would be the first single.

We would need a video clip, and as RooArt were never backward in this area a high-profile director was engaged for the task. The result was a pretty simple but good-looking video. But this sort of quality cost money, and at the end of the process we had spent at least the budget of an entire album on the one video clip. But it didn't matter as the song was looking good for airplay, and we were all convinced we had another hit on our hands.

The next thing was to release 'Monday's Experts' to radio, which was done efficiently enough. And then the next thing was to get the records in the shops, which is where the process started to break down as RooArt had made the decision to distribute the product through Warners — the very same company that had dumped the Weddings after we came back from the US with *The Big Don't Argue*. Even though we'd had a bona fide hit in the interim there wasn't confidence in the band's ability to generate sales.

So, no matter how much our management coerced and cajoled and warned them that the single was indeed getting a ton of attention at radio level, the people who made the decision about pressing the actual product just didn't believe we would sell that many. Even as the song was receiving significant airplay around the country, the shops couldn't actually get a hold of the product. By the time Warners had realised their miscalculation and pressed a new lot of CDs, it had dropped out of the charts entirely. As Triple J had decided they would start playing 'Island of Humour' instead, the single was officially finished. We were stuck with an expensive video clip and a scramble to get 'Island of Humour' released before Triple J stopped playing it. Which I think they did pretty much as soon as it was released.

You would have thought that was it for 'Monday's Experts'. But we hadn't counted on the *Talking Football* program using it as a theme song, which gave it a whole new lease of life, at least in some states, rendering it a quasi-hit. The problem was when it came to paying royalties it hardly registered a blip. This was because Monday night isn't the busiest time for ratings, and whichever channel it was had decided it wasn't an official 'theme song' (theme songs come under a different ruling to normal airplay). But we were convinced it was, and so was everyone connected to the song. Sure enough, when we challenged them with the definition of what constituted a 'theme song' they conceded that it was, and we were due a fair bit of extra money. The problem was they didn't want to pay this much, so they made a counter-offer for use of the tune, which is apparently acceptable practice. We reached a figure that everyone was happy with. So every Monday night for at least half of the year we got to thinking that the song had paid its way handsomely.

That was until after about two or three years, when suddenly another song appeared on the program, which some people thought was reasonably similar to ours — although I thought it wasn't *that* close. The only thing that irked us was that when asked why they had stopped using 'Monday's Experts' the station made a statement to the effect that we had asked too much money, even though we had agreed to the same reduced fee three years running, with never an inflationary index in sight.

By the end of the sorry saga we were left without a whole lot of affection for the song, I'm afraid. But as the years have passed I have felt myself warming to it, and I think there's actually something pretty unassuming and inviting about its compact nature and the directness of the riff that sits under the vocal line. The fact is I haven't got a whole lot of songs like it, and so Wally and myself have come more and more to rely on it as a short, sharp signal that can be thrown in the set nice and early — generally number three or four, after some newer tunes — to say that we will, of course, be playing some of the old stuff. Don't stress — it screams loud and clear. We are going to fulfil our obligations. Which is more than I could say for the industry that created the tune in the first place.

Preceding page left: Anna Burley in the background. Port Fairy Folk Festival, 2010

Preceding page right: The Huskies little league team (I think). Mick bottom row 3rd from the left. Brian Thomas, top row far right. Geelong West Tech Oval

Opposite: WPA at Bluesfest, Byron Bay, 2008. Photo: Unknown photographer

MONDAY'S EXPERTS

M. THOMAS
MUSHROOM MUSIC

*To play this riff slide up to the bass note of the G chord
from one fret below on the bottom string of the guitar.*

(riff)

G / C / | Em D / / |
G / C / | Em D C / |

(Verse)
Monday's experts always know what's best
Always tell you what you should've done
Monday's experts always know what's cooking
How the game was lost and how it could've been won

(chorus)
Am / / / | C / / / | Em / / / | D / / / |
When Monday comes around everyone's an expert in my town

Am / / / | C / / / | Em / / / | D / / / |
(When Monday comes on by everyone's an expert to this guy)

Am / / / | C / / / | Em / / / | D / / / |
(When Monday comes along everyone's an expert on my song)

Monday's experts

(Verse)
See them in the shop see them down the street (Monday Monday)
When I go up the pub it's nearly everyone I meet
Saying I should've done this or I should've done that
But by the time they're finished talking well my beer's getting flat

(chorus)

(mid)
F / / / | C / / / | F / / / | C / / / |
Tuesday Wednesday I don't mind   Thursday Friday   talking blind

F / / / | C / / / | Em / / / | D / / / |
Saturday Sunday not so bad   Monday comes   it drives me mad

Monday's experts talking in the tearoom
In the workshop and the office talking all around the place
Monday's experts yeah they've always got the good oil
Pity you can't put a bet on at the finish of a race

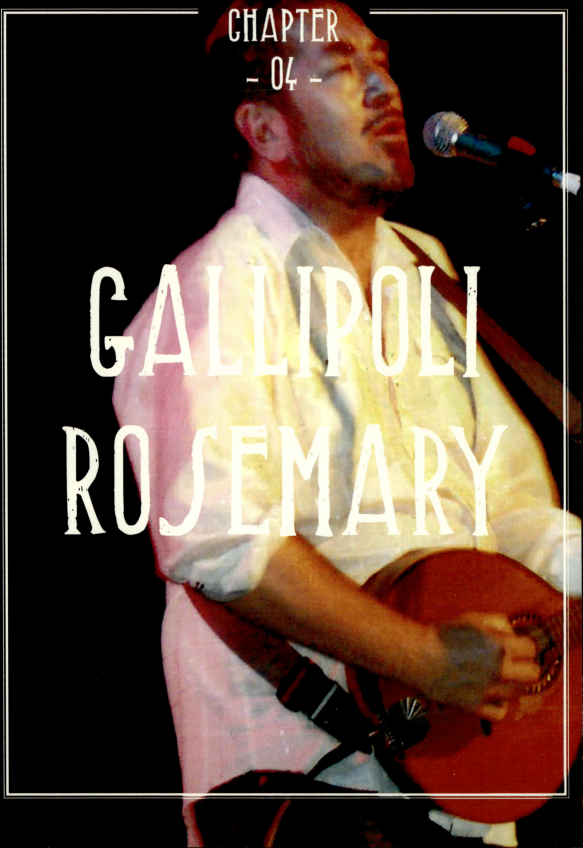

CHAPTER
- 04 -

GALLIPOLI ROSEMARY

I WILL FOREVER ASSOCIATE THIS SONG WITH THE HOUSE AT BEALIBA IN VICTORIA, WHERE IT WAS WRITTEN. WE'D BEEN INTERESTED IN GETTING A WEEKENDER FOR SOME TIME, AND NOTICED IT ADVERTISED FOR SALE ONE DAY IN THE *TRADING POST* NEWSPAPER. IT SEEMED A LITTLE FAR FROM MELBOURNE FOR MY LIKING AND I KNEW NOTHING OF THAT DISTRICT, BUT IT WAS IN OUR PRICE RANGE, SO WE DECIDED TO LOOK ANYWAY. BEFORE WE KNEW IT, WE'D SIGNED THE PAPERS AND THE PLACE WAS OURS

It was a solid old weatherboard building that had originally been the local police station, before being relocated a couple of kilometres from the town centre to its present site in the sixties. It was only when speaking to my brother I discovered this was the same town in which my mother's family had lived for a long time, and that my grandfather and great uncle were supposedly on the town's war memorial. My mother's sister was born there and my grandparents were married in the town down the road.

And so for the next eight years our life was split between Melbourne and this tiny town of eighty souls, two-and-a-half hours to the northwest. We wrote and worked there, had parties and made albums. Other people used it to rehearse, to write, to form new bands and consolidate old ones. *Paddock Buddy* and most of *Spin! Spin! Spin!* were recorded between its warm timber walls.

The rosemary plant in the song was given to me by a friend who proudly told me of its origins growing on the field of battle in Gallipoli. I suppose it was being around the personally relevant war history of the town that made it all the more special to me. The plant must have been from a hardy strain, as the area where we planted it is very drought-prone, and even when we were at the house regularly we weren't the most attentive gardeners. The fact it thrived by the backdoor means it must have wanted to be there in some capacity.

The names on the war memorial I mention, 'carved in marble' and the 'initials fading, fading' are particularly significant in that for a while we had our doubts it was actually the town my maternal grandfather, George Collison, had enlisted from. The only Collisons on the memorial in the main street had the initials 'C' and 'A'. Arthur was his brother's name, but we were baffled by the initial 'C', until my mother noticed that it was a simple error in the re-touching of the marble carving and the letter 'G' was actually still there in relief underneath. So it was from that tiny place the young men of the Loddon had marched away to such an uncertain future. I think this is what the song is driving at — just how tenuous our connections to the past can be, and that something living, be it a plant or a person, is more significant than the grandest of monuments.

Upon returning from the war in Europe, my grandfather had found the town offered nothing much in the way of work, and according to my mother had then been informed by his wife that gold prospecting was no fit occupation for a family man. (It's still a place that attracts prospectors to this day, and there are a number of disused mines on the block where the house is situated.) The family relocated twenty kilometres to Dunolly and ultimately to Melbourne, so it wasn't until my wife Jen and I came up the highway in 2005 that we would again have any association with the place as a family. We sold the house this year, so maybe that's it for that district and our mob. We'll see where the living link will end.

The other thing that makes the song special is I see it as a really significant element in the resumption of my performing with Squeezebox Wally. It came along at a time when we hadn't played together for some years. I think I'd felt after the Weddings it was important for me to be playing with new people, and I wanted to make the statement that it wasn't a direct continuation of that band, with which the sound of the accordion will forever be synonymous. Wally and I had kept in touch, and even managed to find some small spot for the accordion on nearly all the albums I'd released under my own name after 1998. But no, in true Spinal Tap fashion we'd remained firm: 'We shan't be playing together again.'

Preceding page right: The house at Bealiba, Central Victoria

Current page: WPA at The Palace, Melbourne, 2012

And then the WPA reunion shows began in 2008 and I found myself playing alongside the wheezing, huffing, puffing accordion once more. And it felt pretty good. Like all these things, there's always an excuse to keep the thing going a little longer than it should. The Grand Final Eve shows in Melbourne had seemed a good idea the first couple of years after the big tour, and then we got the offer to perform the entire *Scorn of the Women* album at the Enmore Theatre in Sydney, and that'd seemed pretty attractive as well. It was a great show for a lot of reasons, not least that all the significance wasn't being reserved for the Melbourne audience. The Weddings had really worked at being a national (and for a time international) act, so we were chuffed that Sydney was hosting such an occasion for us.

It was around about this time my mother had passed on after a protracted and awful illness. By the time the big show in Sydney was done I think I was performing and operating generally in some sort of haze, and I remember asking Wally if he felt like coming up to play with me at the Bendigo Folk Club the week after. The thought of that long drive on my own was possibly just too much to contemplate at that point.

After the grand statement of the Enmore Theatre it was strange to be driving to Bendigo, where the pair of us played to about sixty people in the room under the grandstand at a local footy club (Sandhurst?). But something really clicked that night, and on 'Gallipoli Rosemary' — which I don't think Wally or anyone else had heard before then — it became evident. He was immediately taken with the song, as were the crowd, and it ended up being a really special show all round.

As we drove the forty minutes to the house in Bealiba, we agreed we'd enjoyed the show every bit as much as the one before it at the Enmore Theatre. 'Gallipoli Rosemary' had been the standout song of the night and, weirdly, it felt like we were starting a band.

It was definitely the first song we recorded for *The Last of the Tourists* in Portland, Oregon. I remember the day being cold and rainy and the studio being warm and friendly, and myself and Wally feeling instantly at home there. We hadn't needed to sound-check for hours and hours before something was ready to go to tape. Darren Hanlon played the bass and I think Adam Selzer did the percussion along with the engineering, and he asked after this pretty early 'take' if we wanted to do another 'take' for safety. I replied that if he thought it was good enough then we'd go with that one, and he seemed pretty relieved that this was the way we would run the session. Down with the second-guessers, I say!

GALLIPOLI ROSEMARY

M. THOMAS
MUSHROOM MUSIC

(intro)
| C / / / | G / / / | Am / / / | Em / / / |
| F / / / | C / / / | F / / / | Am / G / |

(verse)
| C / / / | G / / / | Am / / / | Em / / / |
Gallipoli Rosemary growing in the winter sunshine

| F / / / | C / / / | F / / / | Am / G / |
Out by my back door looking over me and mine

| C / / / | G / / / | Am / / / | Em / / / |
Gallipoli Rosemary for the water and the light you're straining

| F / / / | C / / / | F / / / | Am / G / | F / / / | F / / / |
On the banks of Cochrane's Creek from the shores of the Mediterranean

(chorus)
| F / / / | F / / / |
You grew from a cutting from a bush that grew from a

| F / / / | F / / / | F / / / |
cutting from a bush that grew from a cutting from a bush that drowned in a

| F / G / |
living hell

| F / / / | F / / / | F / / / |
Straggled right back in a ragged rucksack to the bright sunshine from the

| F / / / | F / / / |
old Lone Pine (singing 'Auld Lang Syne')

| F / / / | F / G / |
The living hell of the Dardanelles

(verse)
Gallipoli Rosemary oh hang in there buddy
In the land so parched and dry from a land so torn and muddy
I'm going to put you with a rack of lamb I'm going to cook you in a rabbit stew
Gallipoli Rosemary yeah I got plans for you

GALLIPOLI ROSEMARY

(chorus)

(mid)

| E7 / / / | E7 / / / | F / / / | F / / / |
The young men of the Loddon   the flowers of the forest

| E7 / / / | E7 / / / | F / / / | F / / / |
They carved your name in marble   so you were   not forgotten

| D7 / / / | D7 / / / | F / / / | F / / / |

| E7 / / / | E7 / / / | F / / / | F / / / |
Initials fading fading   until one   day I think

| E7 / / / | E7 / / / | F / / / | F / / / |
A plant by my back door   is the only   living

| D7 / / / | D7 / / / | F / / / | F / / / |
link   The only living

| D7 / / / | D7 / / / | F / / / | F / / / |
link

| F / / / | F / / / |

Gallipoli Rosemary how did it look to them
Walking down the old main road such proud and broken men
They buried you in an old clay pot out in the bed by a willow tree
The second best thing that came back Gallipoli Rosemary
And for the ones did not come back Gallipoli Rosemary

You grew from a cutting from a bush that
Grew from a cutting from a bush that
Grew from a cutting from a bush that
Grew from a cutting from a bush that
Grew from a cutting from a bush that grew…

CHAPTER - 05 -

HARD CURRENCY

I have trouble thinking of the songs we played on that European tour back in 1998.

It was the year before the Weddings officially called it quits (for the first time) and I was struggling with the whole restricted repertoire that our modicum of local success had created. Consequently, I'd chosen to head to Europe with Mark McCartney for six months to simply play as much as possible and see if I could build a new repertoire from scratch. It was a good exercise — creative spring cleaning, in a sense. And I guess there's nothing to make you value your old songs like standing in the corner of a bar in an obscure European pub, having people request 'Brown-Eyed Girl', 'Dirty Old Town' or 'Flower of Scotland'.

When we landed in Amsterdam we began practising right away, and I think there was a fair slather of Hank Williams, Woody Guthrie, Tex Moreton, Townes Van Zandt, Steve Earle and Teenage Fan Club in there to pad out the set. As time went on we added and subtracted tunes, but what interests me are the songs that were written along the way. 'Hard Currency' was most likely the first of these.

The morning it came to me is quite clear — it was on the drive from Vienna to Ostrava in the Czech Republic, with Mark McCartney and WPA merch-person Chelsea Dave Suttee. We were in a VW Wagon of some sort, all happy and expectant as we crossed the border heading off on an adventure. But crossing that border into the towns that make a living servicing the people coming up from more affluent countries was confronting, and I guess what the song is about is what happens when worlds collide.

It stayed with us as a theme over the following weeks and was never too far from our revelry. The last verse comes directly from a night in a little bar way out near the Ukrainian border, as we watched a blinking television advertising all the spoils of Western life amid the squalor and chaos. 'It's just not fucking fair,' Dave Suttee said, and there were really no other words for it.

'Hard Currency' has been in and out of the set over the years, and while I think it's never really found its feet as a live entity, it's a song I feel strongly about. I found myself driving through the Czech Republic once again in 2012 with Squeezebox Wally, and in spite of the new unified currency nothing much appeared to have changed. There was still that desperate sense of one lot of people trying to get a hold of a perceived prosperity others had access to.

No, Dave Suttee said it right back in 1998. It's just not fucking fair.

The recording on this from the *Dust on My Shoes* sessions features a pretty epic line-up of players. Mick O'Connor is on the Hammond organ, Matt Walker on the lap steel, Ray Pereira plays percussion, along with Michael Barclay on drums, and funnily enough Darren Hanlon played the bass (which I find amusing as he was to be the bass player on *The Last of the Tourists* album some fourteen years later).

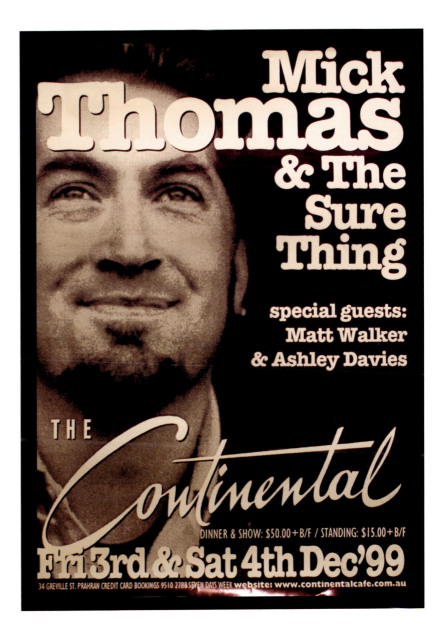

Preceding page left: Mick quayside on the island of Barra. Outer Hebrides, Scotland, 1998

Preceding page right: Mick and Mark McCartney chowing down in rural Austria, 1998

Opposite: Mick and 'Chelsea' Dave Suttie on a tow path. Sonning, England, 2000

M. THOMAS   **HARD CURRENCY**   MUSHROOM MUSIC

(riff)
D / / / | / / / | Em / / / | / / / |
D / / / | / / / | Em / / / | (G) / (B) / |

(verse)
D / / / | / / / | Em / / / | Em / / / |
In a hired car   we drove up to the border

D / / / | D / / / | Em / / / | (G) / (B) / |
They checked our passports there man it was all in order

D / / / | D / / / | Em / / / | Em / / / |
The rain it fell like clockwork the High Tatras shone like tinfoil

D / / / | D / / / | Em / / / | (G) / (B) / |
We laughed to travel so well we drove around a corner

Am / / / | Em / / / | G / / / | G / / / |
And on a roadside there two young girls dressed up and willing

Am / / / | Em / / / | G / / / | G / / / |
A hard life lived in crowns with dreams of dollars deutschmarks shillings

Am / / / | Em / / / | G / / / | G / / / |
Just looking for   looking for a chance to deal in…

(chorus)
D / / / | G / / / | D / / / | G / / / |
Hard   hard   currency feeling

D / / / | G / / / | D / / / | G / / / |
Hard   hard   currency mean and

D / / / | G / / / | D / / / | G / / / |
Hard   hard   currency

HARD CURRENCY

She picked my guidebook up she read down the page then
The bit about her town oh the place that she was raised in
She told me where she worked all about her mum and her dad
She looked back at my guidebook she said Ahhh fuck it's not that bad
Talk turned to other places shiny brighter better billing
Not the place where she cam from what did I care about her feelings?
Just knowing she might never get a chance to deal in

(chorus)

In a tiny bar the television flickered
The drinkers lay about man it looked like a truck had hit them
Outside the snow was falling and ahhh the wind was blowing
And all the years of dirt and drinking could not compete with knowing
Then an add for Pepsi cola made them look and set them reeling
Clean white nymphs on beaches left them with a sinking feeling
Just knowing they would never get a chance to deal in…

(chorus)

(turnaround)
Em / / / | / / / / | A / / / | / / / / |

(chorus)

(over intro riff)
It's a lonely
It's a lonely
It's a lonely
It's a lonely planet

THERE ARE A VARIETY OF REASONS PEOPLE MIGHT LIKE ONE SONG OVER ANOTHER. WHY THEY MIGHT TAKE IT TO HEART AND LET IT BECOME *THEIR* SONG. AND REALLY, PAST A POINT I DON'T THINK IT'S GOOD OR HELPFUL FOR ME TO BE WORRYING TOO MUCH ABOUT IT. WITHOUT TRYING TO SOUND TOO MODEST WE HAVE TO BE SINCERELY GRATEFUL THAT PEOPLE CHOOSE TO BE ENTHUSIASTIC ABOUT OUR MUSIC ON ANY LEVEL. BUT IT IS FASCINATING THE WAY SOME PEOPLE ARE HAPPY TO BECOME KNOWN FOR THEIR INSISTENCE THAT YOU PLAY A PARTICULAR TUNE ON ANY GIVEN NIGHT. SOME A LOT MORE THAN OTHERS, I MIGHT ADD

Karen Hopper loved this song. As a committed long-term supporter of our work with the Weddings, and post WPA, it often seemed to be the one song she wanted to hear. On so many occasions — at the Greendale, at the Corner, at the Caravan, and so many other weird venues that she and her husband Mark resolutely followed us to — it was the one she would politely request. And I always felt it strange that someone from such an obviously supportive and productive marriage, with a generous, ebullient extended family, was drawn to a tale of such a pained dysfunctional domestic situation. But who knows what draws a person to a song?

It wasn't always an easy song to place. For me, it's a weighty piece that doesn't work so well without an introduction. And then to compensate there was the 'set piece' that I worked up, initially with Darren Hanlon, concerning the actors who would play the characters in the fictitious film that never got made that the song was originally based on. At times it seemed as though the introduction was as important as the three verses that make up the actual song, and it seemed to go for a damn site longer than the song itself — which only served to make it even more difficult to position in any given set list. But when we managed to get it in the right place we found it did seem to have a strong effect on people. It certainly seemed that way for Karen.

It is so sad to write that Karen is no longer with us, but I'm really glad to put this song in here and have it on the compilation album as it will always make me think of her. She was someone who treated our music with a load of respect and a gentle resolute enthusiasm, someone who came to a lot of shows.

Guesting on the recording of the track for the *Dust on My Shoes* album were Ed Bates on the pedal steel and Mick O'Connor on the Hammond organ. I think we may have even done a couple of shows with Ed Bates on the steel, but for the most part all the songs from *Dust on My Shoes* were to find their live footing with the basic four-piece band. At various times I have been attracted to the idea of a much larger group, and lamented the situation that you have to make these decisions based purely on logistics and economics. Against that I have often been glad of the trade-off that having limitations can create — different arrangements or people changing instruments or playing parts that they didn't actually play on the album version. Although, I have to say, there's something about hearing these great players together on a track like this that sounds good to my ears all these years later.

Preceding page left: Mick in downtown Melbourne, 2005

Preceding page right: Greendale Hotel. From left: Mick, Rosie Westbrook and Karen Hopper. Greendale, 1999. Photo: Mark Hopper

Opposite: Tour poster, 2013. Design: Jen Huntley

BAKED A CAKE

M. THOMAS
MUSHROOM MUSIC

(riff)
          (GAB)   (CBC)
G / / | / / / | C / / | / / / | Am / / | / / / | Em / / | D / / |

(verse)
G / / | G / / | C / / | C / / | Am / / | Am / / | Em / / | D / / |
  I started to shake I knew it was you   when I heard your footsteps on

   G / / | G / / | C / / | G / / | Am / / | Am / / | Em / / | D / / |
the porch   Then the kids they were starting to laugh. I said 'Nathan don't point

   G / / | G / / | C / / | C / / | Am / / | Am / / | Em / / | D / / |
with your fork.' Then the rain it was starting to fall   I said 'Now you're here come

G / / | G / / | C / / | C / / | Am / / | Am / / | Em / / | D / / |
Inside.' You took off your hat rolled up a smoke. You asked How's it been? I said…

(chorus)
C / / | D / / | G / / | D / / | C / / | C / / | D / / | D / / |
I'd   have baked a   cake   if I   knew you were coming

C / / | D / / | G / / | D / / | C / / | C / / | D / / | / / / |
But   now   that   you're here   it's time we did some talking

C / / | D / / | G / / | D / / | C / / | C / / | D / / | / / / |
Whom I   trying to   kid?   Well I knew you were coming around

(verse)
So come over here stand in the light
And let me get a good look at you
Your hair smells of smoke and your clothes need a wash
Don't think I don't know what you do
In a town such as this well people will talk
If you think you're above it that's fine
But when they ask of you and what I would say
If you turned up I'd say…

BAKED A CAKE

(chorus)

(mid)

Em / / | Em / / | Em / / | D / / | C / / | C / / | C / / | D / / |
                This time of the year   it's getting so

Em / / | Em / / | Em / / | Em / / | Am / / | Am / / | D / / | D / / |
cold   The nights are so long it gets dark so early   these

Em / / | Em / / | Em / / | D / / | C / / | C / / | C / / | D / / |
days   I need somebody here   I need someone to

Em / / | Em / / | Em / / | Em / / | Am / / | Am / / | D / / | / / / |
hold   But I'm feeling strong and don't think I will ask

C / / | D / / | G / / | D / / | C / / | C / / | D / / | / / / |
you to stay -------------   At least not tonight

C / / | D / / | G / / | D / / | C / / | C / / | D / / | D / / |
anyway

C / / | D / / | G / / | D / / | C / / | C / / | D / / | D / / |
I'd   have   baked a   cake if I   knew you were coming

G / / | / / / | C / / | / / / | Am / / | / / / | Em / / | D / / |
around   And I knew you were coming

G / / | / / / | C / / | / / / | Am / / | / / / | Em / / | D / / |
around   And I think that I'm coming

G / / | / / / | C / / | / / / | Am / / | / / / | Em / / | D / / |
around   I want to thank you for coming

G / / | / / / | C / / | / / / | Am / / | / / / | Em / / | D / / | G →
around

HERE'S A PIECE I WROTE FOR THE WEBSITE A COUPLE OF YEARS BACK:

HARD FOUGHT CAREERS: MELBOURNE CONVENTION CENTRE

I PLAYED A STRANGE SHOW TODAY. BUT IT WAS A GOOD SHOW. IF CONNECTING WITH AN AUDIENCE AND FEELING REASSURED PEOPLE FIND MEANING AND SIGNIFICANCE IN YOUR WORK IS THE THING THAT KEEPS YOU PERFORMING THEN IT WAS ALMOST AS GOOD AS IT GETS.

It was one song to a whole lot of people — and I didn't even get to choose as I was booked to play that particular song. That was the deal. I was more than glad to do it because the people at the Australian Nursing Federation said they were still finding inspiration in the song 'Sisters of Mercy' — written about the 1986 nurses strike in Melbourne — and if people are still touched by a song after all this time then I'm all for it. Honoured, in fact.

As I played it was whisper-quiet, and the faces of the audience at the Melbourne Convention Centre were just so intense and focused that the four minutes the song takes seemed to go by in an instant — or an eternity. There was a spontaneous ripple of applause at the line 'blow your horn if you support'. And then it felt like my voice was starting to crack by the second chorus as it just seemed so moving to be playing to the delegates there. To people so intent on fighting for something so fundamental and decent that it's hard to believe the struggle has continued on through all these years.

And as I felt like I might lose my composure it made me focus on something that happened a couple of years ago, when I was performing in a theatre show called *Dust*, written by a Melbourne playwright Donna Jackson (with songs by Mark Seymour). We'd had a fantastic show in Sale and really brought the house down and wrung every last bit of emotion from the piece, which concerned the appalling effect of the asbestos used in all walks of Australian life for so many years. On this night we felt we'd 'nailed it', and with the local choir in full voice had been really happy to see so many people with tears in their eyes. So when the director (also Donna Jackson) came to do the daily critique of the piece for the actors and players (called 'notes' in the theatre world) we were surprised to find her really unhappy with the performance. Totally annoyed, in fact. She explained — it wasn't a 'victim' piece. Not an attempt to illicit cheap emotion or play up to people's sense of sympathy. And apparently, as the person leading the singing I was the chief culprit in this outpouring of emotion. She insisted the play was about people fighting against adversity, about supporting each other and finding strength in dark places.

Music is such an emotive force that it can tend to be a sort of default mechanism for a performer, who spends a lot of time playing to crowds that can be less than attentive, that when a crowd are really connecting with a piece of work you might fall into the trap of going for this heightened melodramatic delivery. So I'd had to sit there and take the criticism in front of the cast of largely amateur local participants, and ultimately conclude she was actually right in her judgement. And here I was, years later in front of over a thousand union delegates, in danger of falling back into the same trap. But they didn't want tears and they didn't want a quavering voice. They wanted exactly what you would think they might want — respect. I finished the song fine, with Donna's diatribe of three years ago still ringing in my ears. Such is the way your thoughts can run during the course of a four-minute song.

After the performance I spent an hour catching up with an old friend from the Sydney rock'n'roll scene of the late eighties. Brett Stevenson has been working for the union for the past five or six years, and had a nice simple way of looking at the work he is doing now compared to the work he did all those years ago. According to him, the real similarity between nursing and music is that they are both professions people undertake because it is something they want to do and that they feel needs to be done — and this is what leaves them wide open to exploitation. It's not a bad way of looking at it, in my eyes. I'm glad I was able to keep my performance in check and really hope I played the song as well as was humanly possible. As I said, I'm honoured to have been a small part of it, even for four intense emotion-charged minutes. I wish everyone there all the best in their ongoing struggle. Hard fought careers indeed …

Preceding page left: A shirt that has lasted a lot longer than a lot of the players, 1995

Preceding page right: The Australian Nurses Federation rally at the Melbourne Convention Centre. Melbourne, 2014

Opposite: Mick outside the customs house. Southwick, England, 1989

M. THOMAS   MUSHROOM MUSIC

Sisters of Mercy

(intro)
Bm / / |D / / |G / / |F#m / / |Em / / |A / / |

Bm / / |D / / |G / / |F#m / / |Em / / |A / / |

(verse)
Bm / / | D / / | G / / | F#m / / |
Oh the winds they were howling   both ragged and cold Through the

G / / | F#m / / | A / / | A / / |
grey Melbourne streets in the pre-Christmas days And the

Bm / / |D / / | G / / | F#m / / |
Sisters of Mercy looked out through their tents   At the

G / / |Bm / / | A / / | A / / |
fires in petrol drums they seemed to say Have

G / / | D / / | G / / |D / / |
we come to this   is it all we can do   To

Bm / / |Em / / | E / / | E / / |
sit here and wait   to see the thing through? But to

G / / | D / / | G / / | D / / |
dig in their heels was a thing they'd been taught   So they

Bm / / |Em / / | A / / | A / / |
painted a sign and it said 'Blow your horn if you support.'

G / / | G / / | C / / | G / / |

(chorus)
A / / | D / / | A / / | D / / |
Oh Sister of Mercy   why can't they see   That a

G / / | D / / | A / / | A / / |
daughter of charity   you'll never be   It's a

SISTERS OF MERCY

A / / | D / / | A / / | D / / |
wicked old game that the government play   When they

G / / | D / / | A / / | Bm / / |
treat you like dogs then you must have your day

(intro)

(verse)
It's a telephone vote so run to your phones
All the people dial in from their luxury homes
It was easy to do far too easily done
Well the thumbs they went down it was three against one
And none of us now can know how that felt
But they strengthened their stance and they tightened their belts
And the papers said no beer this Christmas it seemed such a shame
While the nurses sat out in the wind and the rain

(chorus)

(verse)
Well the girl on the six o'clock news looked concerned
As she told of developments bitter and bold
But I could not help wonder what she got for Christmas
And was there a story she hadn't been told
In the news room at the break up the whole thing was fine
For they never drank beer the bastards drank wine
While down on the pickets they cared not for beer
Just for health just for welfare and just for their hard-fought careers

From left: Mark McCartney, 'Squeezebox' Wally, Shelly Short, Gus Agars, Mick and Laura Jean. Yarra Hotel, 2013. Photo: Mark Hopper

I RECALL DOBE NEWTON FROM THE BUSHWACKERS ASKING THE WEDDINGS TO PLAY A BENEFIT GIG FOR A CAUSE RELATING TO MUSICIANS' HEALTH. IT WAS QUITE EARLY IN OUR CAREER, AND I REMEMBER FEELING PERPLEXED BY THE WHOLE CONCEPT AND SOMEHOW CONFUSED IT WAS EVEN AN ISSUE TO BE ADDRESSED. I MEAN, WASN'T HEALTH JUST AN ISSUE ACROSS THE BOARD, FOR EVERYONE?  I SUPPOSE IT TOOK YEARS TO APPRECIATE JUST HOW DIFFERENT THE LIFESTYLE OF MANY MUSICIANS IS AND HOW DEVASTATING THE WHOLE IDEAL CAN BE; THERE'S SCANT REGARD FOR ANYTHING LIKE SELF-PRESERVATION.

There was, years later, an endless succession of funerals — Steve Connolly, A. P. Johnson, Stewie Speed, Ron Verhoeff, Rob Vela, Janine Hall, Louis McManus. So many that when I sing 'When You Go' I'm hardly sure who initially inspired it. I do recall a sound guy for the Weddings saying offhandedly in reference to the prevalence of suicidal behavior that 'there'd always be a band to see or a game to go to', which is a simple and effective sentiment, I still think. So at least I can locate where some of the song specifically originates.

For the most emotional renditions of the song I'd have to think back to The Sure Thing around the time Stewie Speed joined, and how much the tune meant to him in the wake of his mother's demise. There he was on the side of the stage, singing his guts out about the loss of a loved one, ultimately charging toward his own horrendous finale.

I think the song has always been overshadowed by people's insistence that we keep the WPA tunes 'For a Short Time' and 'Rain in My Heart' in the repertoire, thereby rendering it a little overly morbid in a set already weighed down by anthems to bereavement. Add in the prospect of the occasional desire to play 'In Your Memory', and it was really only a casual inclusion for a couple of years. And still, when I listen to the tunes that made up the album *Dead Set Certainty*, I'm happy I chose to put something really weighty on there.

That album was recorded around 1999, when I was keen not to give too much away in terms of my post-WPA song catalogue. The album began life in my backyard bungalow studio on a single eight-track ADAT recorder. I mixed it out in Warrandyte with Doug Roberts at what was formerly John Farnham's studio, and was feeling really positive by the time it was finished. I'm pretty sure I didn't even go to the trouble of shopping it to any labels, but was happy for it to come out initially on Suitcase Records — a label set up by then-manager Peter Hayes and Mushroom Publishing executive Bill Page. For its second pressing we changed it over to a fledgling Croxton Records, so it's a significant release in one way or another, I suppose.

The band at the time — The Sure Thing Mark I — was just myself, Darren Hanlon and Rosie Westbrook. We hadn't played a lot when we did this recording, and I was firm in the idea that it would be a string band, sans drums. It was probably a couple of rowdy pub shows that changed this; before long Ryan James would be behind the kit, ultimately paving the way for Michael Barclay to return, then Al Barden, then Barclay again.

Preceding page left: Ron Verhoeff at the Café 't Monumentje. The Jordaan, Amsterdam

Preceding page right: From left: Craig Pilkington, Paul Moriaty and Stu Speed. Sanlitun, Beijing, early 2000s

Opposite: Poster for the Paddock Buddy album. Design: Jen Huntley

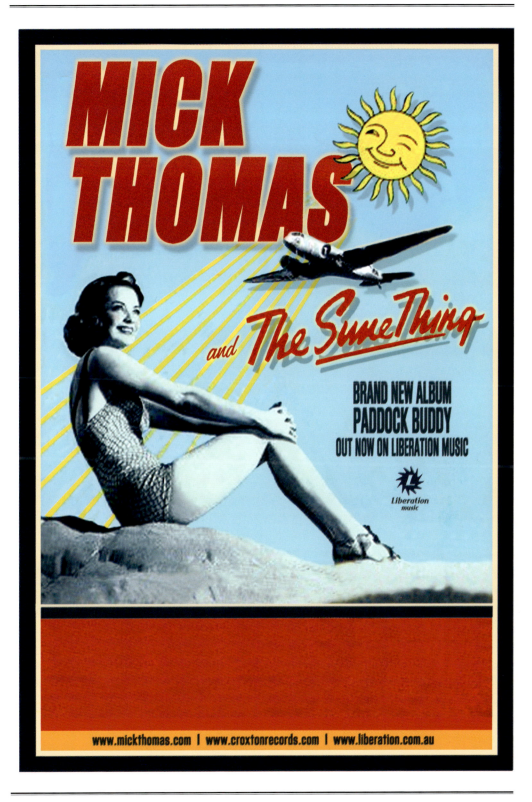

WHEN YOU GO

M. THOMAS
MUSHROOM MUSIC

(verse)

```
       D / / / | D / / / | Em / / / | Em / / / |
When you go we'll burn your body          And a

G / / / | G / / / | Em / / / | D / / / |
toxic cloud will rise above this town  so dark  So what you

       D / / / | D / / / | Em / / / | Em / / / |
got?   You got no takers          Think I might

G / / / | G / / / | Em / / / | D / / / |
take the dogs a-walking down my local park   'Cause there'll
```

(chorus)

```
A / / / | A / / / | F#m / / / | F#m / / / |
always be a band to see a book to read a game to go to

A / / / | A(G) / / / | A(F#) / / / | A(E) / / / |
Songs to write and pools to swim and a dog that needs a ball to throw to

      G / / / | G /(F#) / | Em / / / | Em / / / |
                                  So don't go

D / / / | D / / / | Em / / / | Em / / / |
yet 'cause we're not ready           We're not

G / / / | G / / / | Em / / / | D / / / | D →
finished with you darling by a long shot no
```

(verse)
And when you go we'll all start drinking
Say it's what you would have wanted say it's what you would expect
And late that night we'll get to thinking
It's a mockery a lottery just who goes next

(chorus)

(verse)
And when you're gone and the tears are finished
Will this town be any different will this town be any less
And will your memory be diminished
By the ones who follow after who could try but never guess

(chorus)

The one and only gig of The Van Demons. From left: Ron Verhoeff, Billy Abbott, Mick, Mike Moran and Mark McCartney. Speigeltent, Edinburgh, 1998

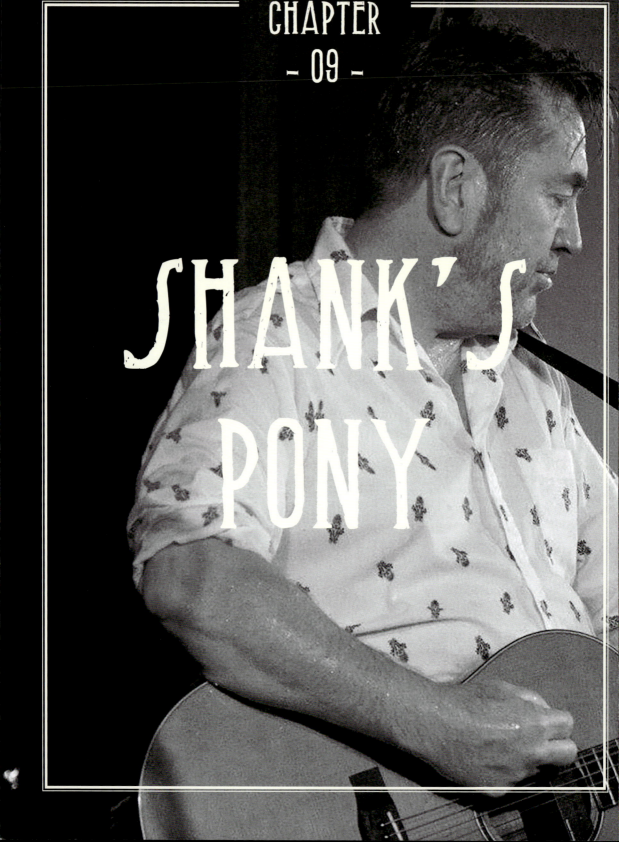

THIS IS ANOTHER OF THE TUNES I CAN REMEMBER PLAYING ON THE EUROPEAN TOUR IN 1998, SO IT'S CERTAINLY ANOTHER OF THE FOUNDATION TUNES I USED WHEN STARTING TO CREATE A LIFE POST-WPA. IT'S A SIMPLE SONG THAT IN ITS ATTEMPT TO SOUND LIKE THE ANDREWS SISTERS PROBABLY PRE-FIGURED MY ENJOYMENT OF CALYPSO MUSIC IN GENERAL.

The recording on *The Horse's Prayer* was done out at Doug Roberts' Clam Shoals Studio in Kangaroo Ground. Although it's a mere hour's drive from the city, we chose to rent a house near the studio so we could dedicate ourselves to the task of what ultimately became a sprawling piece of work. I'm still not sure about double albums generally — we may have been better served by some self-editing. Against that, it was a pretty happy and ambitious band at the time, so I think you just go with it, although in such situations a lot of what you do can feel more profound and important than it actually is.

Whatever the final outcome, I remember it as an enjoyable few weeks creatively, and have great memories of some of the performances on that record. Having Git and Rusty Rich sit in for 'Disrepair', finally getting a solo version of 'Ewan and the Gold' one evening as the sun set over the hills, and just hearing the great Stewie Speed when he was on his game, playing the simplest of things so beautifully.

Looking back, it's hard to fathom that Stewie Speed only played on that one album with The Sure Thing (he also played on the *Liberation Blue* acoustic record). He was such a major presence for us all and his passing seemed so momentous that it feels odd there isn't a more substantial testament to his involvement in our lives. Even when I do remember some great moments in the studio, it only makes me feel cheated that there weren't subsequent albums he could've played on.

As a song to remember him by, 'Shank's Pony' evokes such vivid memories of him walking down Brunswick Street alone on sweltering nights back in the nineties, when we first became acquainted. Spare a thought for the walking wounded indeed …

For the *Horse's Prayer* sessions, The Sure Thing had just settled into what I thought was going to be some sort of enduring line-up. Along with Stewie Speed we had Craig Pilkington and Michael Barclay, and soon it felt like a really even and potentially rewarding group to be playing with. As it goes in this business, you start to make predictions about how good it might get and how long it might last. And then one night during the making of that album, after about a week stuck out in Kangaroo Ground, my partner Jenny came out and we decided to head to the St Andrews Hotel for a counter meal with Michael Barclay.

After dinner, as we walked back to the car we heard a Creedence Clearwater tribute band playing in the lounge, and like some sort of country rock lemmings we paid our $10 and went in. About a month later Michael got an offer to join the Creedence band, so the line-up of The Sure Thing Mark II was already in limbo.

He eventually re-joined the band a couple of years later when Al Barden left and he had tired of playing 'Proud Mary' at far-flung RSL clubs.

Preceding page left: On stage for the Melbourne Folk Club at the Bella Union. Melbourne, 2014. Photo: Mark Hopper

Preceding page right: Mick half way up Ruckers Hill, Northcote. Melbourne, 1998

Opposite: Stu Speed

SHANK'S PONY

M. THOMAS

MUSHROOM MUSIC

(Capo 2nd fret)

(chorus)

| C / / / | Am / / / |

Hey Shank's pony whaddaya know? It's just

| G / / / | Dm / / / |

you and me and a long way to go I said

| C / / / | Am / / / |

Hey Shank's pony whaddaya see? Such a

| G / / / | Dm / / / | Dm(E) / / / | Dm (F) / / / | C / / / |

long way to go and just you and me you and me   you and me…

| Dm / / / | Dm(E) / / / | Dm (F) / / / |

Hey   hey   hey   Well

(verse)

| G / / / | F / C / | G / / / | Dm / / / |

don't look now again it's me well who did you expect to see? Boy

| G / / / | F / C / | Dm / / / | Em / / / |

you can drink and you can talk you missed your ride

| D7 / / / | G / / / |

So you can walk

(chorus)

(verse)
Down London streets we walked in style
On Toronto streets we walked for miles
In Amsterdam I walked with care
You know I didn't even speak
The language there

SHANK'S PONY

(chorus)

(verse)
Well I had a girl and she had me
But we couldn't get on, you know we didn't agree
We did what's right we did what's best
What she's doin' tonight I can only guess
Before I leapt well I never looked
I just dealt out the hurt like a school camp cook
It was lukewarm and late all over the plate
It didn't look pretty
And it didn't taste great…

(mid)

Am / / / | G / / / | F / / / | C / / / |
So spare a thought   for the walking wounded, won't you

F / / / | F / / / | G / / / | G / / / |
While you're driving home tonight   But with

Am / / / | G / / / | F / / / | C / / / |
company like this I could never be marooned and if you

F / / / | / / / | G / / / |
Offered me a lift I'd probably say   I'll be all

F / / / | F (E) / / / | Dm / / / | Dm (E) / / / |
right   I'll be all

F / / / | F (E) / / / | Dm / / / | Dm (E) / / / |
right   I'll be all

F / / / | F (E) / / / | Dm / / / | Dm (E) / / / |
right   I'll be all

F / / / | F (E) / / / | D7 / / / | G / / / |
right

(chorus) x 2

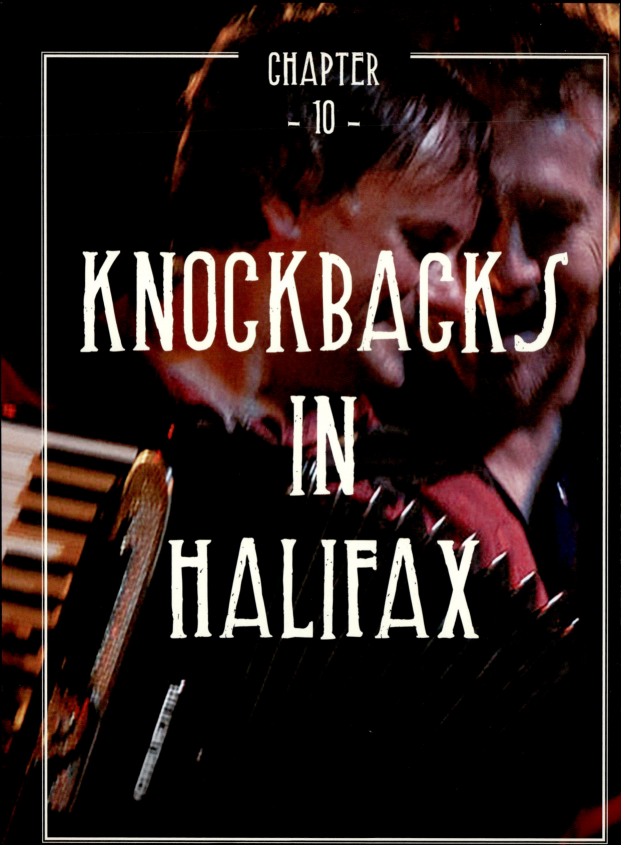

CHAPTER 10

KNOCKBACKS IN HALIFAX

CANADA HAS BEEN PROBLEMATIC FOR ME POST-WPA, AND THAT'S A LITTLE SURPRISING CONSIDERING HOW MUCH TIME WE SPENT THERE IN THE LATE EIGHTIES AND EARLY NINETIES. BUT IT'S REALLY BEEN AT AN INDUSTRY LEVEL THAT THINGS HAVE STALLED, AND THE TIMES I'VE MANAGED TO GET MYSELF BACK THERE IT'S ALWAYS GREAT TO SEE OLD FACES TURNING OUT TO ASK WHAT HAPPENED TO US AFTER 1994. THERE'S BEEN SOME REALLY GOOD SHOWS — JUST NOT ENOUGH OF 'EM.

But in 2012, our friends in the Lowest of the Low came through and invited Squeezebox Wally and myself over to open for them on their Twentieth Anniversary Tour for their landmark album *Shakespeare My Butt*. They played as our backing band each night with Ron Hawkins on bass, so it was a quasi-Weddings sound we were presenting, which was fine by us. Most nights at the merch stand we were signing vinyl albums that were purchased a long time ago.

It was about five weeks in all, and the thing on the itinerary that had us the most excited was a couple of shows in Halifax, Nova Scotia. It was towards the end, so expectation had a chance to build as we contemplated a place that had become almost mythical for us in our twenty-year absence.

It started off well. We flew across Canada on a flashy new boutique airline that left from an airport pretty much in downtown Toronto. We landed and drove into town full of expectation — I think we both wanted to yell, 'Hey, we're the guys from *that* band, who wrote *that* song. Who remembers us?' But we didn't. We sat in the van and bitched about the cold. Because it was cold — cold in a special eastern Canadian way.

The first task we had was a radio interview accompanying the Lowest of the Low. It was a commercial station and the deejay was pretty much uninterested in the two old Aussie guys they had dragged along. Until Ron told him we were the guys that had released *that* song all those years ago. And I think he replied, wondering what song they were talking about, and that it was no use getting too precious about these things as it had been twenty years, and this was a commercial radio station where if you're not a bona fide golden-oldie then they will probably struggle to recall something that occurred last month. But in his polite Canadian way the deejay agreed to let us play *that* song anyway, and so our trip to Halifax a day early was not in vain.

After that we checked in to our hotel and Wally decided to hit the hay early as neither he, nor Ron for that matter, were feeling too good. It had been four weeks touring and we were starting to pass the dreaded lurgies back and forth in the van and the rehearsal room, and in this respect touring has changed little in the last twenty years. I went out with Steve Stanley from the Low and had a nice respectable night checking out a local band, and then back to the hotel in good shape for the next couple of nights.

By the next day Ron had come down with a serious flu and Wally wasn't feeling too good either. The rest of us had lobster for lunch in the Blue Nose Café, which was great and could have been a whole lot more fun if not tempered by the encroaching sickness in the tour party and the responsibility of our show that night. Perhaps it was the sustenance supplied by the lobster, but we held up well and the Lowest of the Low were great as usual. We played *that* song at the end of our set and it got a good response — though I think it's fair to say it wasn't the ecstatic explosion of enthusiasm we'd hoped for. But there were people there that fully remembered what a time we'd had out there so long ago, and you can't argue with someone coming out to support a band that hasn't been through town in twenty years now, can you?

After a few quiet beers with the punters we found ourselves back at the hotel, and everyone was concerned how Ron was faring for the next night's show. They needn't have worried as I think I could have sung their whole set with a fair degree of proficiency, but we all knew it wasn't going to come to that. Still, it didn't make for a buoyant atmosphere in the tour party.

We spent the last day in town wandering the familiar city and the not-so-familiar waterfront market precinct, and the altogether surprising and impressive craft brewery down by the docks. Everyone managed to keep themselves nice in anticipation of the last show that evening. Surely this was going to be the big one.

Once again the crowd was strong, and once again we managed to reconnect with some old faces. But by this stage Wally had come down with a full bout of the dreaded Nova Scotian tour flu as well, and so he was out of the venue as soon as we'd finished. Then Ron and most of the band decided to do the same, and so there I was, standing at the bar with a guy I'd hung out with twenty years ago. He said he knew of a party happening somewhere across the city, and we just needed to find a cab and we'd be there in no time, and the whole thing was suddenly feeling very familiar.

And you know, I honestly would've gone if we'd been able to find a cab, but after waiting forty minutes I decided to accept defeat and head back to the hotel myself. We shook hands and suddenly I was walking through Halifax late on a Saturday night. I was alone, it was freezing, I had nothing at all to drink. As it began to rain I spied a girl selling hotdogs outside a nightclub and I thought, well, someone has got it worse than me. And she sure did look cold, so I thought I'd do the right thing and bought myself a bratwurst or some such — which at that time of the morning is never a good idea. Worse still, as I bit into it a filling at the back of my mouth disintegrated, and it seemed to just get colder and colder as the toothache took hold the further I walked.

Then my phone rang and it was my brother calling from Hobart, and there's nothing like a call from home to make you feel colder, drunker and lonelier than you are already feeling. And so that was Nova Scotia, twenty years on, and if I may be so bold as to quote myself: 'There might be one more drunk in Halifax, but some things never change.'

Preceding page left: Mick and Wally. Photo: Mark Hopper

Preceding page right: Mick and Wally with The Lowest of the Low. Buffalo, USA, 2012

Above: Toronto gig poster 2012. Design: Jen Huntley

KNOCKBACKS IN HALIFAX

M. THOMAS
MUSHROOM MUSIC

(chorus)
```
    G  /  /  /  |G  /  /  /  |G  /  /  /  |G  /  /  /  |
It's Saturday night  ----------------   ----------------   -------------- in

    D  /  /  /  |G  /  /  /  | D  /  /  /  | G  /  /  /  |
Halifax   The kids are out there dancin' it's the same old beat   It's

            D  /  /  /  |A  /  /  /  |A  /  /  /  |
         all over the world           And in her

    G  /  /  /  |G  /  /  /  |G  /  /  /  | G  /  /  /  |
eyes                ----------------   -------------   I could have sworn I saw the

 D  /  /  /  | G  /  /  /  | D  /  /  /  |A  /  /  /  |G  /  /  /  |
northern lights but it was the light flashing from the disco's silver ball
```

(verse)
```
       D  /  /  /  |G  /  /  /  | D  /  /  /  |G  /  /  /  |
I come  ten thousand miles to be here   I can't say that I'm not

   D  /  /  /  |G  /  /  /  | D  /  /  /  |G  / D  /  |A  /  /  /  |
glad   I won't say that it's the best old time that I have ever had       And

        G  /  /  /  |D  /  /  /  | G  /  /  /  | D  /  /  /  |
    sure I'd like to dance my girl but hey not to that song     for I

        G  /  /  /  | D  /  /  /  | G  / D  / |A  /  /  /  |A
    hated it in Sydney          I despised it in Geelong
```

KNOCKBACKS IN HALIFAX

(chorus)

(verse)
You saw me paying for admission saw me looking at my watch
Saw me freezing in my jacket fearful of the cold I'd catch
And I love the Blue-nosed girlies and I love the local beer
When I dance to Whitney Houston I wonder what I'm doing here

(chorus)

(verse)
Hey do you like the clothes I'm wearing or perhaps I could have changed
Do you understand my talking do you think that I talk strange?
But if you can't understand me darling that's not such a shame
'Cause the shit we talk at discos the world over sounds the same

(chorus)

(verse)
It seems now the night is over it seems I've lost my mystique
She got the bloke from Montreal I got a kiss upon the cheek
With a belly full of bitter it's a walk home in the rain
There might be one more drunk in Halifax but some things never change

(chorus)

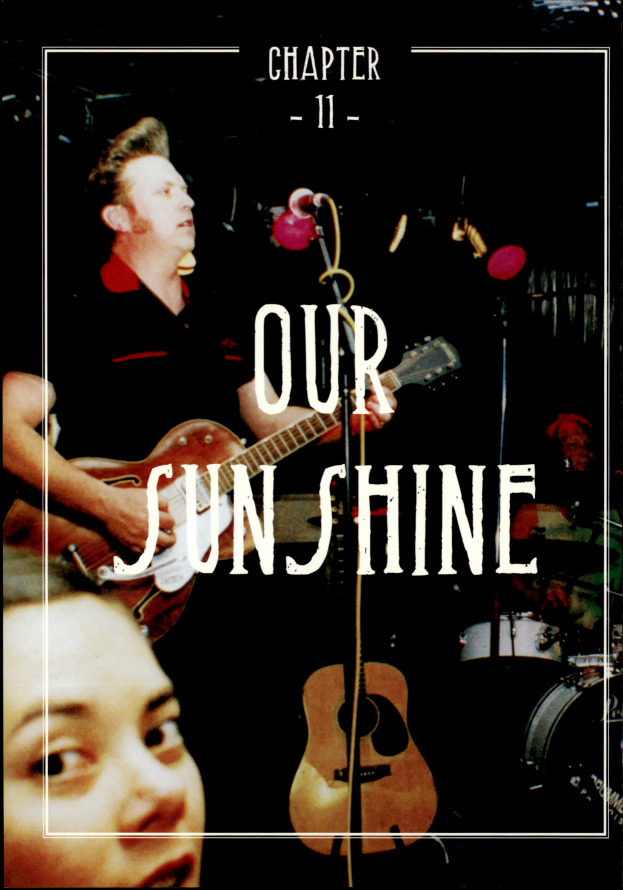

IN AMERICA THERE SEEMS TO BE A MUCH GREATER STRESS PLACED ON CO-WRITING, AS RECORD COMPANIES TRY TO WRING FULL VALUE OUT OF WRITERS WHO OFTEN NEED THE COERCION TO BECOME PRODUCTIVE. BUT INITIALLY I FELT THAT I WAS SIGNED WITH A FULL COMPLEMENT OF SONGS AND THAT SHOULD'VE BEEN ENOUGH. OVER THE COURSE OF MY CAREER THIS HAS CHANGED A LOT AS OPPORTUNITIES HAVE ARISEN TO MEET AND WORK WITH A WIDE VARIETY OF PEOPLE (AND, OF COURSE, AS IT'S BECOME EVIDENT THAT INITIAL COMPLEMENT OF SONGS WOULDN'T LAST FOREVER).

I recall Paul Kelly asking me quite early on if I had anything unfinished he could have a look at, and I thought little of it at the time. But suddenly you find yourself a decade down the track, and having been through some bleak periods where the songs have dried up, the chance to sit down and write with someone you have the utmost respect for comes along, and obviously you jump at it.

'Our Sunshine' was written at a house up in Mount Macedon at a Mushroom Music songwriters' retreat, and came from the fact both Paul and I had recently read the Robert Drewe book of the same name. Without much available extra information concerning the exploits of Ned Kelly and his gang (this was pre-internet), we reverted to a book of Australian paintings that contained the Sidney Nolan *Ned Kelly* series. It's fair to say the song became more about the legend than the actual reality — or at least about the Nolan paintings themselves.

I'm pretty sure Paul had most of the tune and a good half of the lyrics by the time I became involved and started adding anything of an equestrian nature I could think of, but that's the way it goes with co-writing. It's not a quantitative exercise — the short line to finish off a verse, the extra chord in the chorus, the repeated phrase at the play-out could be the thing that makes the song what it is.

When I was writing the song 'Calling Me Home' with Sara Storer and Trey Bruce (at yet another of the Mushroom Music songwriter junkets) I became conscious the chorus has a weird gap in it after the sixth line. At the time I felt it desperately needed to be filled, but Trey was adamant it was fine as it stood. Listening to it now I know he was totally right; the oddness of this little gap is one of the really endearing elements of the chorus. That song and 'Our Sunshine' are probably my two most commercially successful songs post-WPA, so perhaps co-writing is something I should be doing more of.

The song has been a live staple for me since it was written. I think the fact it has been covered by a variety of people over the years, as well as being a regular inclusion in Paul Kelly's various line-ups, means it almost qualifies as a hit tune for a lot of people less familiar with my entire catalogue. It was one of the first songs we recorded for *The Horse's Prayer*, meaning the line-up was Michael Barclay, Stewie Speed, and Craig Pilkington, who also constructed and played the whole signature mariachi trumpet section.

Preceding page left: Craig Pilkington and Michael Barclay at The Evelyn Hotel, Fitzroy. Melbourne, early 2000s. Photo: Mark Hopper

Preceding page right: Paul Kelly with WPA at Central Club Hotel, Richmond. Melbourne, late 1990s

Opposite left: Stu Speed, Mick and Craig Pilkington on the Great Wall of China, early 2000s

Opposite right: Mick and Stu Speed at the Corner Hotel, Richmond. Photo: Mark Hopper

Above: Lino cut by Mick. Design: Jen Huntley

M. THOMAS (MUSHROOM MUSIC) P. KELLY (SONY/ATV)

OUR SUNSHINE

(intro)
| Dm / / / | Dm / / / | Dm / / / | Dm / / / |
| Dm / / / | Dm / / / | Dm / / / | Dm / / / |

(verse)
| Dm / / / | Dm / / / | Dm / / / | C / / / |
Well there came a man on a stolen horse and he rode right onto the page

| C / / / | C / / / | C / / / | Dm / / / |
Burning bright but not for long lit up with a holy rage   No

| Dm / / / | Dm / / / | Dm / / / | C / / / |
turning back for a child of grace with the blood red on his hands

| C / / / | C / / / | C / / / | Dm / / / |
Never known to hurt a woman   never hurt an honest man

| Bb / / / | Bb / / / | C / / / | C / / / |
Mother gone to gaol his father dead

| Bb / / / | F / / / | F / / / | C / / / | C / / / |
and daily rising   the price upon his head

OUR SUNSHINE

(chorus)
Dm / / / | Dm / / / | C / / / | C / / / | Dm / / / | Dm / / / | Dm / / / | Dm / / / |
Our Sunshine --

Dm / / / | Dm / / / | C / / / | C / / / | Dm / / / | Dm / / / |
Our Sunshine ---

Bb / / / | Bb / / / | F / / / | F / / / |
Through fire and flood   through dust and mud

C / / / | C / / / | Dm / / / | Dm / / / | Dm / / / | Dm / / / |
Through the tears and blood keep riding on
        (repeat final two lines an extra time each chorus)

(verse)
Forever trapped in a suit of steel with the hotel burning behind
Betrayed by his companions and a train waiting down the line
Forever caught on a barebacked horse getting through by the skin of his teeth
One more for the ladies one more for the police
Riding all night hungry tired and cold
Into the misty morning you'll never grow old

Bb / / / | Bb / / / | C / / / | C / / / |
As he stood before the judge's chair   he said My

Bb / / / | F / / / | F / / / | C / / / | C / / / |
mind is free and easy   I'll see you there…

(chorus)

CHAPTER
- 12 -

STEP IN
STEP OUT

THIS SONG WILL FOREVER BE BOUND WITH MEMORIES OF THE HOPETOUN HOTEL, SURRY HILLS, SYDNEY, WHERE IT WAS WRITTEN. WHEN YOU START IN BANDS YOU ALWAYS HEAR STORIES OF FAMOUS VENUES — THE HEYDAY OF THIS OR THAT HOTEL OR BAR. SOMETIMES THEY BECOME ASSOCIATED WITH A FAMOUS LIVE ALBUM OR A BAND THAT GOES ON TO STARDOM. SOMETIMES THEY ARE ANALOGOUS TO A MUSICAL SCENE THAT IS CONSIDERED SIGNIFICANT OR IMPORTANT.

By the time the Weddings were really getting started there didn't seem to be anywhere in Melbourne like this for us. The venues where we had found support were ones we had to run ourselves, and the St Kilda scene at the time (The Prince of Wales, The Esplanade Hotel, The Seaview Ballroom, etc.) didn't really have much interest in a bunch of daggy boys from north of the river. But the Hopetoun was different entirely, and from the moment we went there we felt welcome and valued as a band.

I am pretty sure we played there on our first proper tour of Sydney. We had the good fortune to be opening for Stevie Ray Vaughan at the Hordern Pavilion, which was our Saturday show taken care of — and so our first actual pub gig in Sydney was on a Sunday evening at the hallowed Hopetoun. I think we finished our run there on a Sunday pretty much every time we went to Sydney for a long time after that.

My memory is of wild shows, long shows, sweaty shows — the heat a formidable thing to experience for boys from Melbourne. Coming out after a big chaotic encore and seeing various band members and road crew all slumped on the burning concrete of the four corners of Fitzroy and Bourke Street is an image burnt in my memory.

As regards 'Step in Step Out', it must've been our third or fourth trip up the highway as we had become very familiar with the Hopetoun. Some of us were already staying upstairs in anticipation of our move to the Harbour City. The Coloured Girls (Messengers) had been living there until then, and as they moved into more substantial permanent lodgings we were only too glad to take over their rooms and rent. They were a friendly lot who worked, lived and socialised there, and I still have friends from that hotel, from that time, some thirty years later.

I have a feeling the song was written on a Monday after a weekend of playing. I know somebody must have had the keys to one of the rooms upstairs, as somewhere in the middle of the revelry, occasioned by a night off in Sydney, I found myself feeling anxious and lonely and happy to extricate myself from the party. And so, with the same mandolin I am still playing to this day, I snuck off and lay my weary head down on the pub bed. But my rest and relaxation was to be short-lived, as the idea for a new song presented itself forcibly, insistently. From memory it came about easily and quickly, and in my opinion still sounds best played on a mandolin — on that one in particular. On that night, to celebrate I took the trusty $200 Giannini mandolin and re-joined the party downstairs. I played the song to everyone in the bar — a few times, I fear. And the party continued on its merry way, for some years after that, I also fear.

By the late eighties the pendulum seemed to have swung back to Melbourne, in particular the inner north. As the band members all drifted home I have a strong memory of the Weddings' manager saying that The Punter's Club was the Melbourne equivalent of the Hopetoun, and maybe he was right as I ended up living there as well after a short stint upstairs at the Annandale Hotel before I left Sydney.

I played the Hopetoun with Michael Barclay the last week of its existence in 2009, and it was a sad place by then. The downstairs bar stank like a bad night-market toilet. The staff were jaded and rude, and I'm not sure why they even asked me to do the show in the first place. If it was for old time's sake then there wasn't too much acknowledgement of its significance and a correspondingly meagre turnout of possible old faces. When someone down in Melbourne wrote something about it being the end for the place it was met with a fairly strong chorus of people who had a fair disdain for the poor old Hopetoun.

The lesson I take from it is that a lot of venues have their time, their heyday, and if you were lucky enough to be there that is well and good, but we should be looking towards the next one as the *really* significant one. Vale Hopetoun Hotel. I loved you well (and at least I got a song out of it).

Preceding page right: Hopetoun Hotel, Surry Hills

Opposite: Punters Club Hotel, Fitzroy

STEP IN STEP OUT

M. THOMAS
MUSHROOM MUSIC

(intro)
G / / / |G / F#m / |A / / / |A / F#m / |
G / / / |G / F#m / |A / / / |A / F#m / |

(verse)
G / / / |D / / / | A / / / |D / / / |
In the morning when from slumber you awake

G / / / |D / / / |F#m / / / |A / / / |
Find me sleeping like a baby by your side

G / / / |D / / / | A / / / |D / / / |
Get up get off to work 'cause there are cakes that must be baked But if there's

G / / / |D / / / |A / / / |A / / / |
things that I must do   I'd sooner let them slide

(chorus)
Bm / / / |A / / / | Bm / / / |A / / / |
And you step out   when I step in   It is a

G / / / |D / / / | A / / / |D / / / |
dance that is bizarre   it is a dance that's wearing thin And you step

Bm / / / |A / / / | Bm / / / |A / / / |
in   when I step out   Though we can't

G / / / |D / / / |A / F#m / |G / / /|
find the time for talking seems we find the time to shout

STEP IN STEP OUT

(intro)

(verse)
And late at night when I come fumbling for my keys
The house is dark and all is quiet (shhh)
Get into bed it is so hard for me to please
You're barely hours away from work and you're so tired

(chorus)

(verse)
Some people pray for rain some people pray for holidays
And some people pray for money without shelter
But we just pray for two shifts at the same end of the day
And a life that is not quite so helter-skelter

(chorus)

G / F#m / |A / / / |A / F#m / | G / / / |
You   and   me been living in different worlds

G / F#m / |A / / / |A / F#m / | G / / / |
You   and   me been living in different worlds

G / F#m / |A / / / |A / F#m / | G / / / |
You and me we've been living in different worlds

G / F#m / |A / / / |A / / / | Bm / / / |A / / / |
You and me

Bm / / / |A / / / |Bm / / / |A / / / | Bm

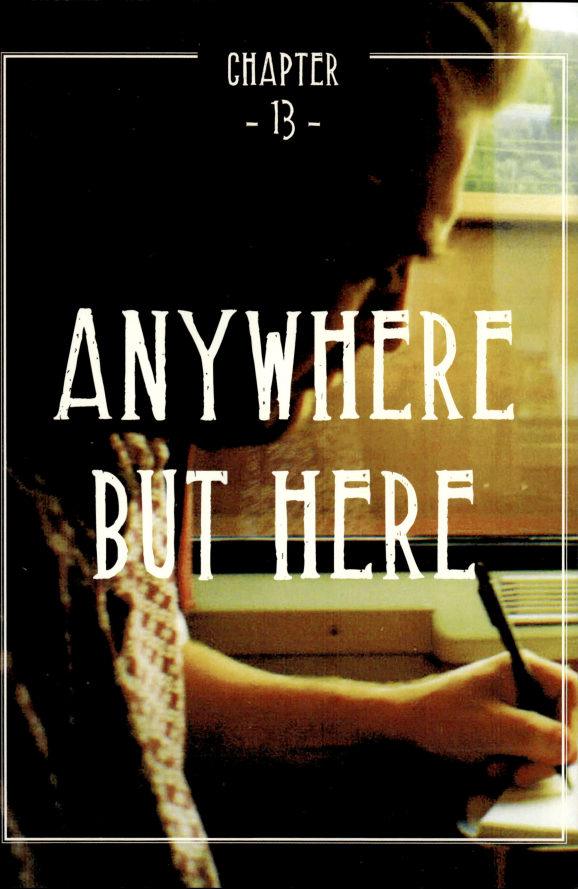

SOMETIMES I THINK IT WAS DUST ON MY SHOES AND SOMETIMES I'M SURE IT WAS ANYWHERE BUT HERE — BUT I'M CERTAIN AT LEAST ONE OF THOSE TWO BOOKS BY PETER PINNEY WAS THE FIRST I LAID EYES ON. (YES, I STOLE THE NAME DUST ON MY SHOES FOR MY FIRST POST-WPA ALBUM).

I know it was the morning after the last show the Weddings played in Warrnambool in southwest Victoria, and we were scouring the op shops with the Waifs. I remember thinking there was something so inviting about the dust jacket, so storybook and old-world, and I was hooked immediately into Peter Pinney's wild ride. And so, while Jen Anderson, Vicki and Donna were trying on old clothes, I was finding something quite fitting for myself.

It's been easy enough to find the rest of Pinney's catalogue, as in his day he was a successful and widely read author. His books are everywhere. *Anywhere But Here* is pretty special for me, though. The thing that makes it really satisfying to read is the subtext of the girl that he follows across Africa. His relationship with Anna somehow never becomes permanent, and as a reader you are always left wondering. It's a lovely story for what it doesn't say.

My brother Steve's company Roar Film put together a *Dust on My Shoes* website for the ABC some years back. It was an epic presentation that chronicled the life and times of Pinney himself, leading the viewer through a bunch of countries he visited — both historically, and in real time in the modern era. Kavisha Mazzella and I wrote a dozen songs for it, and I'm sure it'll find its way onto an album and a theatre stage sooner or later.

One of the strange things that happened once the website started to appear in monthly instalments was we received an email from Holland, from a woman who claimed to have travelled extensively with Pinney in Africa back in the forties and fifties, saying how it was fantastic we were paying tribute to his life and travels. When we checked the name, you guessed it — it was none other than the elusive Anna herself, speaking to us from across the years, across the world. Well, Utrecht actually. I immediately replied, saying that I was going to be in Holland in a couple of months, and would I be able to meet with her and maybe hear some more of Pinney's travels in Africa? But she quickly claimed she had to go to Canada and just didn't seem keen on taking the situation any further. Anna indeed — elusive to the end.

'Anywhere But Here' was originally recorded by Jerry Boys for the *Dust on My Shoes* album sessions, but didn't survive the cut. I think it became a bit of a live staple for a time there, and so we resurrected the band track for *The Horse's Prayer*, meaning it's the only track Darren Hanlon and Craig Pilkington ever played on together.

Preceding page left: Mick on the train somewhere in Europe, 1998. Pre iPad. Glorious.

Preceding page right: Mick playing Katie Fitzgerald's. Stourbridge, England, 2007

Opposite: Poster for Mick Thomas and the Sure Thing gig, 1999. Design: Jen Huntley

Mick in Stonetown, Zanzibar, 2016. Photo: Mark Hopper

ANYWHERE BUT HERE

M. THOMAS

MUSHROOM MUSIC

(riff)

```
Em  /  A   |D / G  |Em  /  A   |D  /  /  / |
Em  /  A   |D / G  |Em  /  A   |D  /  /  / |
Bm  /  /  /  |A  /  /  /  |Em  /  /  /  |A  /  /  /  |
G   /  /  /  |C  /  /  /  |C#  /  /  /  |C#  /  /  /  |
```

(verse)

```
G  /  A  /  |F#m  /  G  /  |G  /  A  /  |F#m  /  G  / |
```
Up the coast and down the coast as long as the coast was clear

```
G  /  A  /  |F#m  /  G  /  |Em  /  /  /  |A  /  /  /  |
```
From Mozambique to the Ivory Coast anywhere but here

```
G  /  A  /  |F#m  /  G  /  |G  /  A  /  |F#m  /  G  / |
```
Saw her in a marketplace   I'd not seen her for years   Then we

```
G  /  A  /  |F#m  /  G  /  |Em  /  /  /  |A  /  /  /  |
```
crossed the border headed north north to anywhere but here

(chorus)

```
Em  /  A  |D / G  |Em  /  A  |D  /  /  / |
```
　　　　　　　　　Hey -----　　　　Anna

```
Em  /  A  |D / G  |Em  /  A  |D  /  /  / |
```
　　　　　　　　　Hey -----　　　　Anna

```
Bm  /  /  /  |A  /  /  /  |Em  /  /  /  |A  /  /  / |
```
　　　　　　　At our age　　　　　　at our stage

```
G  /  /  /  |C  /  /  /  |C#  /  /  /  |C#  /  /  /  |
```
After all this time

(verse)

We ate the fish we ate the rice drank the local beer
We worked a while and then moved on on to anywhere but here
She left me in Monrovia to sail a stormy sea
And she set her sail for Amsterdam and anyone but me

(extra verse bit)

```
Em  /  /  /  |A  /  /  /  |Em  /  /  /  |A  /  /  /  |
```
　　　Anyone　but　me　　　　　anywhere but here

(chorus)
Playout over first half of the chorus

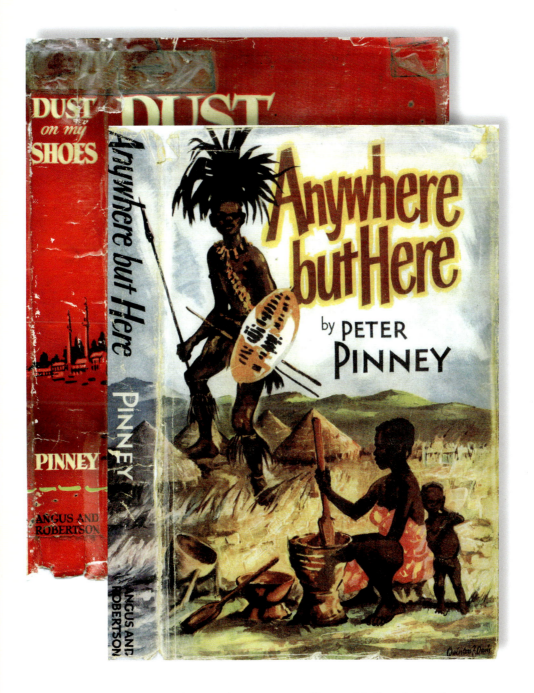

Original dust jackets from Anywhere But Here *and* Dust on My Shoes *by Peter Pinney*

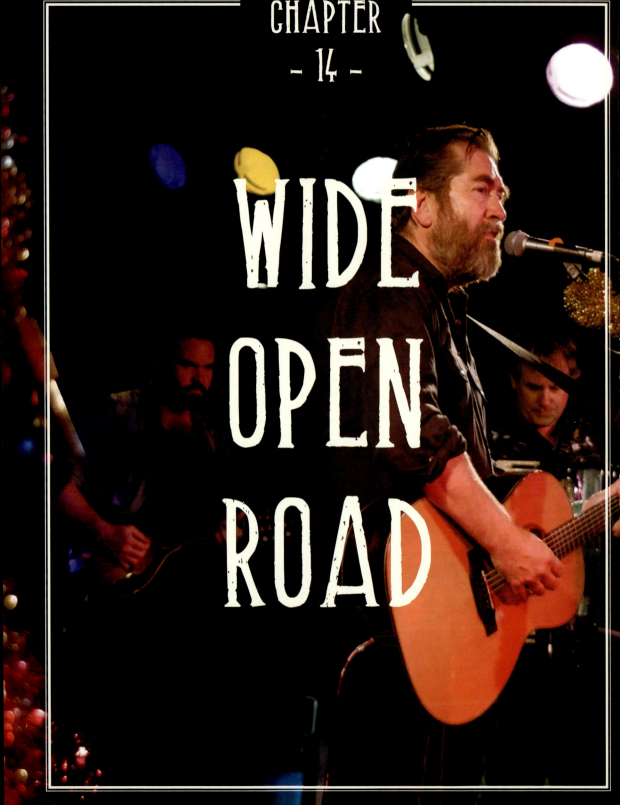

I'VE SPENT THE MORNING UNSUCCESSFULLY SCOURING THE HOUSE FOR A PARTICULAR TRIFFIDS ALBUM CALLED *IN THE PINES*. ON THE BACK COVER I RECALL A PICTURE OF THE BAND ON A DUSTY ROAD IN WHAT I ASSUME IS SOMEWHERE IN WESTERN AUSTRALIA. THAT ALBUM WAS RECORDED IN A WOOLSHED IN A PLACE I'D NEVER HEARD OF, AND IT PROBABLY HAD AS BIG AN INFLUENCE ON ME AS SOME OF THEIR MORE COMMERCIALLY DRIVEN BIG-BUDGET RECORDS. EVEN THE HELL-BENT, INDUSTRY-DRIVEN MANAGEMENT WE HAD IN THE WEDDINGS COULD SEE THE VIRTUE IN ALTERNATING OUR EVER-MORE TROUBLED AND EXPENSIVE ASSAULTS ON THE CHARTS WITH MORE CREATIVE AND INFORMAL RELEASES. OF WHICH *IN THE PINES* IS A CLASSIC EXAMPLE.

It's a great photo, and even though it's on the album that came after *Born Sandy Devotional* it's the one that screams 'Wide Open Road' to me. I don't think we ever drove down to that part of the world without listening to something by them. And although the use of the words 'wide open road' in the song itself could be argued to be more allegorical than anything whenever I sing it, I still can't help but think of that black and white picture and the red dusty wide open roads of Western Australia.

Playing covers was a big part of what the Weddings did. It was there from the start as we fleshed out our set with songs not written by myself: Bob Dylan, Tex Moreton, The Byrds, Chuck Berry, Little Murders, Little Heroes — and of course The Triffids. Later, when Dave Steel joined, it was Neil Young, The Dingoes and Doug Sahm, and then Pete Lawler brought Sam Cooke and a dozen other things we'd never heard of. It took pressure off me as principle songwriter, and most importantly it was a good way of learning some of the vagaries of the art form.

As part of what I saw as the folk music tradition we were often prepared to throw in a song we hardly knew, thinking this was the path to an altogether inspired and original adaptation of an idea. But the longer I have played the less defensible this is as a way of working. It is possibly the internet that has scuttled this, with the problem now being to make sure someone else online hasn't gotten it wrong. Someone on a dodgy lyric website, or someone posting a rough version on YouTube. Your mistakes and mondegreens should be your own, at the very least.

I only ever briefly spoke with Dave McComb about our version of the song. He told me he was really chuffed and quite moved by the experience of walking past a pub in Perth one day, hearing a bunch of people drunkenly singing along to our version. I was glad and relieved for his gracious support, as you are never sure how these things will be interpreted. I hope he meant it.

When someone takes on another person's song an expression often used is 'they made it their own', and I think it's fair to say after playing 'Wide Open Road' for as long as we have it's difficult to not feel some sort of ownership. At Mushroom Records' 25th Anniversary concert at the Melbourne Cricket Ground, Chris Bailey and Paul Kelly performed a version of the song, and later The Church had a crack at it as well. Each time, I had to remind myself it wasn't actually our song in the first place and that the beauty of it is its simplicity — both musically and lyrically. Which is what makes it so transportable. If that's what I felt then I'm not sure what David McComb really thought about our version. But at least they all got the words right.

And I'm damned if I can find that album — and that photo — anywhere.

Preceding page left: Nick O'Mara, Mick and Wally at the Corner Hotel, Richmond. Melbourne, 2013. Photo: Mark Hopper

Preceding page right: WPA outside of Derby, Western Australia. Photo: Matthew Sleeth

Opposite: Mick and Jac Tonks. Corner Hotel, Richmond, 2013. Photo: Mark Hopper

Following page: Doorway sign. North Melbourne, 2016

WIDE OPEN ROAD

D. McCOMB   MUSHROOM MUSIC

(for an intro just strum the chords from the verse)

(verse)

| G / / / | G / / / | C / / / | G / / / |

Well the drums rolled off in my forehead the drums rolled off in my chest Remember (the guns went)

| Em / / / | Em / / / | Am / / / | Am / / / |

carryin' the baby just for you cryin' in the wilderness   I lost

| G / / / | G / / / | C / / / | G / / / |

track of my friends lost my kin cut them off as limbs   And I (crossed them off my list)

| Em / / / | Em / / / | Am / / / | Am / / / |

drove out over the flatland   huntin' down you and him Well the

| G / / / | G / / / | C / / / | G / / / |

sky was big and empty   my chest filled to explode   And I

| Em / / / | Em / / / | Am / / / | Am / / / |

yelled my insides out at the sun at the wide open road

(chorus): same chords as verse

It's a wide open road it's a wide open road
(And now you can go any place that you want to go)

How do you think it feels sleeping by yourself
When the one you love the one you love is with someone else

(chorus)

| G / / / | G / / / | G / / / | G / / / |

Then I wake up in the   morning thinking I'm still by your side

| G / / / | G / / / | Am / / / | Am / / / |

I reach out just to   touch you and it's   then I   realise

(chorus)

CHAPTER - 15 -

FORGOT SHE WAS BEAUTIFUL
(MEMORIES OF TAILEM BEND)

JONATHAN RICHMAN — NOW THERE WAS A CONFRONTING ISSUE FOR A COUPLE OF PEOPLE TRYING TO FORGE NEW CAREERS IN THE CONTEMPORARY MUSIC INDUSTRY. DARREN HANLON WAS ALL FOR THE MAN (I SUPPOSE AS PART OF THE CANDLE RECORDS MOB IT WOULD'VE BEEN HARD NOT TO SALUTE HIM AS AN ARTIST). ME, I WASN'T SO SURE. I HAD BAD MEMORIES OF THE TIME JONATHON RICHMAN FIRST CAME TO MELBOURNE IN THE EIGHTIES. HE'D SEEMED WILFULLY WEIRD AND DEMANDING IN AN UNATTRACTIVE FASHION BACK THEN, AND I COULDN'T SEE ANY EVIDENCE THAT HE MIGHT HAVE CHANGED. DARREN WAS FOREVER ASKING ME IF I HAD HEARD THIS SONG, OR THAT SONG, OR IF I WAS AWARE OF A PARTICULAR ALBUM OR IF I HAD SEEN THAT FILM — BUT IT FELL ON DEAF EARS THE WAY IT OFTEN DOES WHEN SOMEONE IS TRYING TO FORCE YOU TO LIKE SOMETHING

But finally there we were, on my first full national Australian tour post-Weddings, Parties, Anything. We'd played a show in Adelaide at the Governor Hindmarsh Hotel, and with bassist Rosie Westbrook and the sound person taking the hire car, Darren and I found ourselves in my old red Ford driving back down the Western Highway. And did Darren have a CD to play me? You bet he did. That's right, Jonathan Richman was pretty much it for that trip.

The whole day is quite memorable, actually. We'd received a tip for a horserace at the show the night before from an elated punter who, being a massive Simpletons and WPA fan, couldn't believe his luck at finding Darren and myself playing together. Strangely enough, he'd been good to his word and the horse had won at decent odds, meaning we had to detour to collect our winnings before leaving the state.

I remember distinctly the town we stopped in was Tailem Bend. I can remember this because as we were standing at a counter in a takeaway shop waiting for our food, we noticed a small sad-looking book displayed on the counter. It was a local history of the town, titled *Tailem Bend: A Town Searching for an Identity*. Simultaneously, it struck us as the funniest name for a local history we'd ever seen. It was all we could do to keep straight faces, collect our fried morsels and get back to the car without cracking up. A couple of years later when Darren tracked the book down as a fortieth birthday present, I actually waded through it, and found it sad and whimsical in a defeated kind of way … though possibly not one of the great reads of the last fifty years.

Maybe it was the thought of that book title that put us in a strange, contemplative mood, but as the miles fell away and we listened to more and more of dear Jonathan I guess I found myself softening and falling under some sort of spell.

Eventually, as we chatted into the night the way a new band might do on a long road trip, the subject of a mutual friend's relationship bust-up was raised. Darren couldn't believe the guy in question had let the woman go so easily, and I guess logically enough he was referring to the fact she'd be considered really attractive. I replied that if you had to live with her you might soon forget she was beautiful.

Darren seized on this line and this thought. 'Just like a Jonathon Richman song!' he said, and began doing a pretty fair impersonation of the man performing a trumped-up parody of an imaginary song. He was just joking around, but I was sitting behind the wheel thinking that it was actually a pretty fair idea for a tune.

It was years later that I first played him the finished song, by which time he'd totally forgotten his role in its gestation — but it's one that's served me well over the miles. It's a pity we don't do the big drives so much these days. I have quite a few Jonathan Richman albums that I'd love to have the time to listen to. And I'm sure Tailem Bend is still there, searching for an identity.

'Forgot She Was Beautiful' was recorded in a house up at Bealiba in Victoria, and I think it was one of the songs we felt particularly precious about as we had quite a few tries over the week that album took to record. It was Craig Pilkington on guitar, Al Barden on drums and Rory Boast on bass. It was a fun session.

After a hard day recording it was fantastic to wander down to Evans Hotel and talk to the farmers about cantankerous machines — even if ours happened to be an eighties Tascam 1" 16-track tape machine, as opposed to a John Deer Harvester.

The Wilson Pickers' second album had a song on it called 'Tailem Bend', which has no direct connection to 'Forgot She Was Beautiful' at all.

Preceding page left: Darren Hanlon and Mick at the Greendale Hotel. Greendale, 1999. Photo: Mark Hopper

Preceding page right: Darren Hanlon and Sas in Northcote. Melbourne, 2014

Opposite: Shelley Short searches for a town's identity, 2012. Photo: Mick

M. THOMAS

FORGOT SHE WAS BEAUTIFUL

MUSHROOM MUSIC

(capo on 2nd fret)

(intro)
Bm / A / | G / / / | G / / / | G / / / |
Bm / A / | G / / / | G / / / | G / / / |

(verse)
D / / / | G / / / | A / / / | D / / / |
She walked in   he just said   hello She walked

D / / / | G / / / | A / / / | D / / / |
by   they watched as she   did go   Then

G / / / | A / / / | D / / / | G / / / |
his mate leaned across   gave his hand a pat   He

G / / / | A / / / | D / / / | G / / / |
whispered in his shell like pink   Man who the fuck was that?

G / / / | Bm / / / | Bm / / / | A / / / | A →
(Who the fuck was that?)

Well he just smiled and he shook his head
No-one much least not these days he said.
Then he looked at his mate and he said Hey how's about a drink?
His mate said She's a goddess
And he said Yeah d'ya think?
(Do you really think?)

(chorus)
D / / / | G / / / | A / / / | Bm / / / | Bm / / / |
'Cause he forgot   she was   beautiful

Em / / / | Em / / / | G / / / | A / / / |
All those years of putting up and being dutiful

D / / / | G / / / | A / / / | Bm / / / | Bm / / / | A / / / | A →
He forgot   she was   beautiful

FORGOT SHE WAS BEAUTIFUL

(verse)
She came over she sat across from them
She raised her glass up to the pair of them
Well his mate he was stunned he just sat there for a while
Well are you gunna introduce us? he said with a smile
(And I think she liked his style)

(chorus)

(verse)
As they talked was like he wasn't even there
He did not even register she'd changed the colour of her hair
And if she dressed better these days it meant nothing much to him
If beauty is its own revenge she'd never looked so grim
(It meant nothing much to him)

(different verse at the end)

Em / / / | Em / / / | G / / / | G / / / |
All those years of trying for something he couldn't be it When

Em / / / | Em / / / | G / / / | G / / / |
he looked at her now well you know he just couldn't see it See she'd

Em / / / | G / / / | Em / / / | G / / / |
always had that smile   she'd always been that slim She was

Em / / / | Em / / / | G / / / | G / / / | A / / / | A →
beautiful to everybody   everybody in the room but him 'Cause he

G / / / | A / / / | Bm / A / | G / / / | G / / / |
forgot   she was beautiful   She was

Bm / A / | G / / / | G / / / |
beautiful   She was so

Bm / A / | G / / / | G / / / | D →
beautiful

CHAPTER
- 16 -

THE BALLAD OF PEGGY AND COL

I HAD GOTTEN MARK WALLACE'S PHONE NUMBER BY RINGING AROUND TO A FEW MELBOURNE ACCORDION SCHOOLS. I SENT HIM A LETTER WITH A CASSETTE TAPE OF SOME DEMOS WE HAD MADE WITH A FLEDGLING WPA LINE-UP IN 1984. CHADSTONE, WHERE HE LIVED, SEEMED A LONG WAY IN THOSE DAYS.

The date on the front of the letter is 13 February 1985. Which seemed late by my reckoning, in that by 1987 we were signed to Warners and set to release *Scorn of the Women*, and touring nationally. But I guess for a while things moved pretty quickly, and we were very impatient for things to happen. So every week of every month seemed to have its own themes, problems and sense of resolution.

I recall I was supposed to attend Wally's twenty-first birthday party, which would have been towards the end of that year. I got side-tracked down in Carlton, and have always felt guilty I didn't make it. Funnily enough, a twenty-first had seemed like something the younger kids were doing — I would have been all of a ripe old twenty-five years at the time.

The first time Wally came to my house in Brunswick to audition he played me the tune that was ultimately to become 'Peggy and Col'. I think it's fair to say he got the gig, and it's nice to have the song back in the set after all these years.

Preceding page left: Mick and Wally at Song Bingo Session, Kew RSL. Melbourne, 2013. Photo: Mark Hopper

Preceding page right: Mick and Wally, sometime last century

Above: WPA at the Central Club, Richmond when the stage was still on the south side of the room. This makes it about 1990. Photo: Mark Hopper

Opposite: Actual letter Mick wrote to Wally to save driving from Carlton to Chadstone

Following page: Mick and Wally in the late 80s

Mark,

It turned out easier to post the tape than to drop it round. Don't worry if the quality is not too crash hot. It is an old tape — not much top end or anything else for that matter. It should give you an idea of what the band is on about.

The last two songs are demos that I recorded on a home studio with me playing an old accordion. They are pretty rough but will perhaps give you an idea of how we think an accordion could work. Excuse my primative playing!

Songs are as follows: Industrial Town, Water Supply, Evry Where I Go, Streets of Forbes } Weddings, Parties, Anything

Say the Word, Talk Forever } Michael Thomas

All these songs were written by myself except "Streets of Forbes" (traditional)

Hope to hear from you soon.

Michael Thomas
Ph. 3877625

M. THOMAS (MUSHROOM MUSIC)

THE BALLAD OF PEGGY AND COL

M. WALLACE (CONTROL)

(verse)

Gm / Gm (F#bass) / | Gm (F bass) / Gm / |Cm / / / | D7 / / / |
Peggy's been into town been walking   around   drinking with the boys

Gm / Gm (F#bass) / | Gm (F bass) / Gm / |Cm / / / | D7 / / / |
Been spending some money on herself for a change been making so much noise

G7 / / / | G7 / / / | Cm / G7 / | Cm / / / |
Col just sits on a bus to Perth he's got tears in his eyes

F7 / / / | F7 / / / | Bb7 / / / | A7 / D7 / |
Twenty years gone down the drain now the world just passes by

(verse)
She's done up her hair she's gone and bought a new dress
Don't she look a sight
She's been to a party to a rest-ta-ra-raunt
And Peggy feels all right
But Col's been drinking way too hard
He's got bags beneath his eyes
Ten bucks left no job no wife
It's enough to make you cry

(verse)
Now when Col came in he was a dreadful mess
And the kids they just stared blank
He had dirt on his face he had holes in his shoes
And not one penny in the bank
(Meanwhile) Peg was with her man in town
All dressed up like a doll
But she drops it all she goes running home ('Cause when it)

(different ending in the third verse)
Bb7 / / / | D7 / Gm / | Cm / / / | D7 / Gm / |
all boiled down to it Peggy loved Col When it all came down to it Peggy loved Col

Mick and Wally at Greendale Hotel. Greendale, 2015. Photo: Mark Hopper

CHAPTER
- 17 -

MALTBY BY-PASS

THE THING ABOUT SONGS IS, AT THEIR BEST THEY'RE ACCURATE TO A FEELING OR AN EMOTION, AND THIS MEANS QUITE OFTEN THEIR HISTORICAL AUTHENTICITY ENDS UP BEING QUESTIONABLE.

❦

SURELY, IF A SONG CARRIES AN ACTUAL IMPACT IN TERMS OF ITS PERSONAL CONTENT, THEN TECHNICAL VERACITY IS LESS THAN CRUCIAL? I'VE HAD PEOPLE COME UP TO ME AND ASK WHETHER I KNEW THAT EIGHT PRISONERS ESCAPED FROM PORT ARTHUR PRISON AND NOT SIX, AS PER 'A TALE THEY WON'T BELIEVE'? AND OF COURSE I KNOW THAT, OF COURSE I READ THAT IN *THE FATAL SHORE*. BUT SIX JUST FITTED BETTER. IT MADE FOR A BETTER SONG, A MORE SINGABLE SONG, AND THEREFORE THE ACTUAL NUMBER (AS FAR AS I'M CONCERNED) BECAME LESS IMPORTANT

And so it goes with a lot of my songs, 'Maltby By-Pass' being one of them.

When I look at the facts versus the fiction, it's already quite a muddle. I do know that as a family we broke down somewhere around the Maltby By-Pass one time and I'm pretty sure it was in the seventies, seeing as we moved to Geelong in 1969 and I'd left home by 1978. I know that at one stage we owned an EK Holden that was powder blue, although there's a strong chance the car we owned after that — an awful-coloured light-fawn HR Holden — could also have been the vehicle in question. And seeing as we changed over cars soon after moving to Geelong this is possibly more likely.

I also know that the HR came with the job my father had taken with the SEC (State Electricity Commission, back when Australia still had an idea these utilities were too important to be in the hands of private companies) that had moved us to Geelong. As the HR was manufactured between 1966 and 1968 this may have been more likely, *except* …

if it was his 'work car' there's no way my father would've had us travelling in it recreationally, and so the EK still may have been the offending vehicle, *except* … I remember Dad ultimately purchasing the HR from the SEC, as these vehicles were made available to employees at a reduced rate once their tenure with the Commission was over.

So, in all likelihood it was the light-fawn HR and not the powder blue EK wagon that I sing of in the song. But ask yourself which one sounds the best, evokes the strongest memory of a certain time and a long-forgotten past, and I think the EK wagon is the winner.

The next part of the song that needs clarification concerns the involvement of the man in black himself. Did Johnny Cash have his photo taken at the Maltby By-Pass, as I suggest in the song?

Well, if you look at the cover shot on the album *American Recordings*, it's certainly a possibility. It's a very Australian-looking scene — the foliage is typically dry and gnarled in a familiar kind of way. And the dogs in the photo appear to be some sort of Australian sheep dog, to my eye. So I wonder at the story itself.

I don't remember exactly when, how or who, but I was told it one night, somewhere, by someone, and I guess after looking at that picture a bell went off that said of course the photo was taken in Australia. But was he in the van with the other members of The Highwaymen? I doubt musicians who'd been in the business as long as those guys would be hanging around for a photoshoot they weren't even part of. But it's a chance, if they were on their way down to play in Geelong … it's a chance.

I trawled the internet many times to find information about this apocryphal photoshoot and one time managed to find a detailed account of it. Since then it seems to have disappeared, and so I'm left with the faint memory that it was the station master at Little River who owned the dogs. That Johnny Cash named them Sin and Redemption (when their real names were probably Dipper and Scratcher). That they were on their way to a show in Geelong with The Highwaymen …

But I guess the things I do know for sure are that my father left this world the same day Johnny Cash did, and that he was a lifelong fan. I do know that he had a longing for the open road, barely satisfied by our infrequent family jaunts up the Hume, the Newell or the Western Highways. I do know that whatever he felt in terms of his personal longing for freedom, the sense of duty he felt for the job at hand, was profound and unwavering. So I reckon overall, in terms of accuracy the song is (pretty much) spot-on.

'Maltby By-Pass' was recorded in the house up at Bealiba, and beyond the Sure Thing

line-up for that year (Pilkington, Boast, Barden) it featured Chris Altmann on pedal steel, and Barb Waters and Anna Burley on backing vocals (who actually also sang on 'Rain in My Heart' for the Weddings a long time before that). I remember sitting up with Craig listening to *Harvest* by Neil Young the night before we recorded it. Can you tell? I can tell.

Preceding page left: John Bedggood, Mick and Wally do Song Bingo at The Caravan Club. Melbourne, 2011. Photo: Mark Hopper

Preceding page right: Mick and Pa Collison, late 1960s. The car on the left possibly is the car from the song.

Opposite: Mick with Finley and Dulcie. Bealiba, 2008

Above: Finley in the Big Blue Bent Bungalow Studio. See the tapes sitting on top of the harmonium? Those are two forms of archaic music technology right there

MALTBY BY-PASS

M. THOMAS
MUSHROOM MUSIC

(capo 2nd fret)

(riff)
D / / / | A / Em / | D / / / | A / Em / |

(verse)
D / / / | A / | Em / / / | G / |
On a road well travelled on a road well paved   There's no

D / / / | A / | Em / / / (| Em /|) G / |
sun-bleached bones nor unmarked graves   Just a

D / / / | A / | Em / / / | G / |
market garden and a   mountain view   Where the

D / / / | A / | Em / / / | G / |
photographer said John this'll do   They left

A / / / | G / D / | A / / / | G / D / |
Willy and Waylon waiting in the van Willy and Waylon waiting on the man For the

A / / / | Em / | G / / / | G / / / |
light to fade for the camera crew   Ahhh

G / / / | A / | D / / / | A / Em / | D / / / | A / Em / |
c'mon John there's work to do

    Back in the early seventies
    On the very same road past Werribee
    Our car broke down with the holiday load
    Down on the Maltby By-Pass road
    They left us kids all waiting by the van
    Waiting on the lost fifth highwayman
    In an EK wagon powder blue
    Don't bug me kids there's work to do.

MALTBY BY-PASS

(mid)
Bm / / / | Bm / / / | Em / / / | Em / / / |
Take the dog for a walk now kids but mind don't stray too far (there's work to do)

Bm / / / | Bm / / / | G / / / | A / (G) / | (F#) / (E) / |
he sighed out of frustration he crawled underneath the car   That old

A / (G) / | (F#) / (E) / | A / (G) / | (F#) / (E) / |
car   The old blue car   Damn that blue

A / (G) / | (F#) / (E) / |
car

(verse)
To an identical end from a different start
They travelled down the same road they were a world apart
And there's a lesson they taught and I'll tell you it
See you can drive 'round Werribee but you never get past the shit
You leave Willy and Waylon waiting by the van
Waiting on the lost fifth highwayman
In an EK wagon powder blue
Ahhh c'mon boys there's work to do

G / / / | A / D / |
C'mon kids there's work to do

G / / / | A / D / |
C'mon John there's work to do

CHAPTER
- 18 -

A TALE THEY WON'T BELIEVE

HERE'S A PIECE I WROTE FOR THE WEBSITE BACK IN 2009 ABOUT JIM DICKINSON, THE MAN WHO PRODUCED *THE BIG DON'T ARGUE*, AND WHO ARGUED AGAINST CUTTING THE LENGTH OF 'A TALE THEY WON'T BELIEVE', SAYING THE LENGTH OF THE SONG WAS ITS STRONG POINT. *NOBODY*, HE SAID, WOULD BE INTERESTED IN A THREE-MINUTE SONG ABOUT CANNIBALISM!

It was selfish but when I first heard Jim Dickinson was dead all I could think of was that I had lost the chance to go back to Memphis and work with the guy. I had been in touch with him six months back via email, and he was as friendly and cordial as ever. We discussed him mixing the album I had recorded with Nick Barker, and he seemed as enthused and inspired as the person I had last dealt with about twenty years ago. If it seems a little surreal that this potential creative resource no longer exists, I think it's because there was a timeless quality to the way he went about making music. He was as much about respect as he was about iconoclasm, as much for the old guys he had known as for the mavericks coming through. Now he is no longer there to challenge and confound expectations.

My first encounter with him happened in the late eighties, when Weddings, Parties, Anything were looking for a producer for our third album. The first two had been hard enough and only rescued from complete chaos and implosion by the neverending patience of Alan Thorn. By the end of that decade Dave Steel had left the group, and with Warners still firmly committed to the band it was time to throw our net a little wider. Time to get an American producer.

Preferring the higher pursuits of literature, drinking and football, the Weds had no idea about producers — so we got a friend to make a list of prospective people. Jim Dickinson was at the top of the list, and so I went into Waterfront Records in Sydney and they stocked me up with the Replacements, Alex Chilton, Ry Cooder, Green on Red, The Cramps and Mojo Nixon. He sure sounded like the bloke for us. Then one sunny afternoon in Sydney the phone rang and Jim's cracked old voice came through on the other end. Someone from Warners had sent him our first two albums and he was right up for it. The thing that had swung him was an adaptation of a Bertold Brecht poem called 'The Infanticide of Marie Farrar' — so maybe our 'higher pursuits' stood for something after all. We were going to America!

When I had first landed in Memphis he took great care to introduce me around to all the luminaries there — this person had worked with Jerry Lee, this one with The Everlys, this one with Elvis. When the band turned up he took us straight to Sam Phillips Studio to cut some demos with Roland Janes. He was very keen for us to see that music wasn't created in a vacuum.

He always said he found it strange that a band like us had been signed to Warners in the first place, and when the representatives from the American side of the label came down to visit our session at Ardent Studios he was quick to point out that he had a reputation for 'chewing the legs off the recording console'. But somehow he was still as charming as could be with them and avoided direct confrontation. Again, here was another paradox of the man — that he could on one hand be so radical and abrasive creatively, and yet so personable in the way he sold it to the people signing the cheques. It was a big lesson.

We finished the album (*The Big Don't Argue*), the record company ultimately didn't think much of it, and when it didn't yield the hits we had been chasing our days at Warners were numbered. Rather than see it as an unsuccessful mission, I think it was working with a person like Jim that gave me a sense of confidence and a faith in the potential purity of the recording experience that still fuels what I do. Possibly the biggest accolade I can take from that album is Jim's decision to cover one of the songs on a solo record twenty years later ('No, No Never Again' on *Killers From Space*, 2007).

As we left Memphis full of hope and youthful optimism I remember Jim saying to me, 'Don't let the bastards grind you down.' Somehow I think he had an inkling of what was to come with Warners. Within six months I had the humiliating task of having to ring him to get pointless remixes done of a single he didn't particularly want to do. (He said he found singles a pointless exercise for bands like us.)

From the start he maintained it was obscene that any one album could sell millions of copies, and that he was happy enough to plough his own piece of dirt. I guess that piece of dirt was Memphis and I suppose time will only tell how deep the furrow was. He had no shortage of bands who didn't sell a million. Sincere condolences go out to his family — Mary Lindsay, Cody, Luther.

Preceding page left: Mick with the old faithful Telecaster. There's still yellow paint on it (these days wood grain), which puts the photo somewhere before 1996

Preceding page right: Jim Dickinson from when he recorded the Weddings in Memphis, 1989

Opposite: WPA in Memphis 1989. From left: Richard Burgman, Wally, Pete Lawler, Jim Dickinson, Mick and Marcus Schintler

A TALE THEY WON'T BELIEVE

M. THOMAS　　　　　　　　　　　　　　　　　　　　　　　　MUSHROOM MUSIC

(riff)

Em / D / | C / D | Em / D / | C / D |
Em / D / | C / D | Em / D / | C / D |

(verse)

Em / / / | Em / / / | Em / / / | Em / / / |
Well we left Macquarie Harbour   it was in the pouring rain

Em / / / | Em / / / | D / / / | D / / / |
None of us quite sure if we would see England   again   and

C / / / | D / / / | Em / / / | Em / / / |
Some fool muttered   death or liberty   Now there were

Em / / / | Em / / / | Em / / / | Em / / / |
six of us   together   a   jolly   hungry   crew

Em / / / | Em / / / | D / / / | D / / / |
And as the days went by you know our hunger quickly grew and

C / / / | D / / / | Em / / / | Em / / / |
Some fool muttered death or liberty   So that

Am / / / | B7 / / / | Em / / / | Em / / / |
night we made fires out of   twigs and out of bark   And our

Am / / / | B7 / / / | Em / / / | Em / / / |
Stomachs they were rumbling all through the night so dark

Am / / / | B7 / / / | Am / / / | B7 / / / |
Wondering   trying   to keep ourselves alive And when the

Am / / / | B7 / / / | Am / / / | B7 / / / |
sun came up next morning well the six had turned to five (so we said)

(chorus)

Em / D | C / D | Em / D / | C / D |
Right there's another one don't you frown   Chew the meat and hold it down

Em / D / | C / | D / / / | D / / / | D / / / | D / |
for it's a tale they won't believe   When I get down to Hobart Town

(verse)

Well the five of us were nervous and I tell you that's a fact
For you should have seen the bastard who was carrying the axe
He was a sick man he had murder in his heart
And when we reached the Franklin River it took two days to cross
We were wet and we were starving and for food were at a loss
We were hungry we had murder on our mind
And so that night we made fires out of twigs and out of bark
And our stomachs they were rumbling all through the night so dark

They were making noises the deaf could not ignore
And when the sun came up next morning well the five had turned to four

(chorus)
(verse)
The four of us kept on marching to a place called Western Tiers
A country full of tasty game for us it lent no cheer
We had no guns we were travelling without hope
But the axe it loomed so ominous God's hand was at play
For a sick man is a type of game which cannot run away
Stay easy my good man your time's at hand
And so that night we made fires out of twigs and out of bark
And our stomachs they were rumbling all through the night so dark
I can't say that I feel guilty 'cause after all it wasn't me
But when the sun came up next morning well the four had turned to three

(chorus)
(verse)
Well the three of us kept on moving but one was fading fast
He had been bitten by a snake and you could see he wouldn't last
Stay easy my good man your time's at hand
And when he could march no longer his time had come at last
We were far too weak to carry him subsistence it comes first
Stay easy my good man your time's at hand
And so that night we made fires out of twigs and out of bark
And our stomachs they were rumbling all through the night so dark
It was a messy job but it was one we had to do
And when the sun came up next morning well the three had turned to two

(chorus)
(verse)
Now he had been looking at me funny sort of eyeing me for days
And you would not need to be too bright to know that bastard's ways
He was a sick man he had murder in his heart
But even bastards have to rest and even bastards have to sleep
And when he was in the land of nod straight over I did creep
And the axe that he had wielded was all mine
And so that night we made fires out of twigs and out of bark
And our stomachs they were rumbling all through the night so dark
I can't say that I enjoyed it and it wasn't exactly fun
But when the sun came up next morning well the two had turned to one

(chorus)
(verse)
Well now history is a pack of lies as any fool can tell
And when I got down to Hobart Town I told my story well
Do you think they would believe one word I said
For they thought that I was covering for my mates still at large
Said they'd be roaming in the bush so wild and free
And back to old Macquarie Harbour they sent me
But I remembered the fires out of twigs and out of bark
How our stomachs they were rumbling all through the night so dark
And this young fool he just said to me 'Hey it's liberty or death.'
And he looks a rather tasty one so this time I'll go north (and I'm singing)

(chorus)

WE ARE FOREVER BEING ASKED WHAT A SONG MIGHT MEAN —WHAT WE ARE GETTING AT WHEN THE WORDS SAY A CERTAIN THING. AND I'M FOREVER EXPLAINING THEM AWAY, TELLING STORIES THAT MIGHT HOPEFULLY GET THE LISTENER SOMEWHERE CLOSE TO WHERE THE SONG WAS CONCEIVED. BUT ONCE A SONG IS RELEASED IT QUITE RIGHTLY HAS A LIFE OF ITS OWN AND, BARRING THE USE OF A TUNE FOR SOMEONE ELSE'S AGENDA, BE IT COMMERCIAL OR POLITICAL, I THINK IT'S REASONABLE THAT PEOPLE TAKE A SONG HOWEVER IT AFFECTS THEM.

So while people are often quite prepared to list some amusing mishearings of lyrics, or mondegreens, I am much more interested in how far from the original intent a song lyric might be interpreted. Sort of a conceptual mondegreen, you might call it.

When the odious One Nation political party chose Bruce Woodley and Dobe Newton's 'I Am Australian' for one of their early public rallies they were obviously thinking of nothing much beyond the title, and I think the writers were totally within their rights to ask the song be withdrawn from the official campaign. (I'd even go as far as to say the lyrics are diametrically opposed to the whole One Nation platform.) The same goes for Springsteen's 'Born in the USA' when it was hijacked by Ronald Reagan's Republican Party in 1984. But unless someone is using the song to actually profit from it, then it's pretty much a harmless exercise whatever an individual wants to take away.

I recall visiting my father in hospital towards the end of his life. He had been there a while and was glad to see me. He excitedly called the nurses over to explain to them that I was his son and that I was a working musician. He even went so far as to ask if any of them knew the song 'Father's Day'. A few of them said they did, although I'm not sure if they were just being polite as it had been years since I'd had anything much in the way of airplay.

Well guess what, he told them, that song was about him! That long-gone hit tune was all about him and me, he reckoned. And once they'd all nodded enthusiastically and looked suitably impressed I quietly explained to him that the song wasn't really about him, and that I'd written it about a friend's relationship breakdown and subsequent parental difficulties. But no, he was adamant. I was his son, the song was called 'Father's Day', and therefore as far as he was concerned it was about him.

And really, it didn't take too much of a leap of faith to conclude that if that was how he wanted to see it then I was more than happy he got something so positive from it. Maybe he hadn't gotten too much past the title and the chorus of the song, but that's fine if that's how he heard it.

With some songs the story behind them might feel quite involved and crucial to the overall understanding. As if the experience of the listener is in some way compromised if the background isn't conveyed. And there certainly have been times in my career when I have been at great pains to make the background to a tune as plain as I could possibly make it. But the longer I continue to write and perform the more I am happy to let people make of them what they will.

For the twenty years after 'Father's Day' was released I wasn't actually a father myself, something that seemed to surprise a lot of people. But as my father would be quick to point out, I was still a son. And as I would also point out, the pain of being separated from a loved one by circumstance is something that anyone can feel, and most likely where the song derives its potency.

Our manager at the time the tune was released said we were a walk-up start for airplay as seemingly nearly every radio programmer in the country was a divorced father. But I have to say that this is hopelessly cynical, and I have to believe it is the transportable emotion of the tune that has made it one of my most enduring songs. And so I think my father is probably right — it's about him.

Preceding page left: A picture of Jim Armstrong that was on the original cover of the Father's Day single. He's considerably older now

Preceding page right: Mick with his Dad. Weeroona Avenue, Hamlyn Heights, Geelong, 1970

Opposite: Stan Armstrong checks the mics with some help from his son George. Queens Park, Moonee Ponds

Right: WPA setlist with three songs from King Tide meaning it was around 1993–94

FATHER'S DAY

M. THOMAS

MUSHROOM MUSIC

(intro)

| E / / / | A / / B | E / / / | F#m / / A |
| E / / / | A / / B | E / / / | F#m / / A |

(Verse)

E / / / | A / / B |
I haven't always been a single man

E / / / | F#m / / A |
And I haven't always lived up here

E / / / | A / / B |
Along with all these other single men

E / / / | F#m / / A |
With a ring around the bath and a cigarette butt in my beer

E / / / | A / / B |
And I haven't always been a lonely man

E / / / | F#m / / A |
And I haven't always lived alone

E / / / | A / / B |
And you know I haven't always drunk this much

E / / / | F#7 / / / |
But hey before you cut me down just try standing in my shoes

A / / / | A / / / |
'Cause I don't have to hear one word of this no

(chorus)

E / / / | F#7 / / / |
On any other day   I might care what you say

A / / / | A / / / |
But every Saturday is   Father's Day

E / / / | F#7 / / / |
And you might call it sad and you might call me mad

A / (G#) / | F#m / / / | E / / / |
But I've got one   who calls me   dad (back to opening riff)

(verse)
And all the other blokes that live up here
Know how to leave a man alone
They're not a bad old bunch that live up here
Ah but you know that it's not family and it's not home
What of the darling wife that once I had?
Well I'm pleased to say that she still talks to me
But I try not to think of what went wrong
'Cause if I said that I was right
She might say that she was right
And the only rights I care about are visiting rights yeah

(mid)

| D / / / | D / / / | E / / / | E / / / |

We go where he wants to go   We do what he wants to

| D / / / | D / / / | E / B / | F#m / / / |

do   I tell him everything I know 'Cause I'd do anything to prove

| E / B / | F#m / / / |

Yeah I'd do anything to prove

(extended chorus)

| E / / / | F#7 / / / |

On any other day   I might care what you say

| A / / / | A / / / |

But every Saturday is   Father's Day

| E / / / | F#7 / / / |

And you might call it sad and you might call me mad

| A / / / | A / / / |

But it don't feel so bad   when he calls me

| E / / / | F#7 / / / |

And you might call it sad and you might call me mad

| A / / / | A / / / |

But it don't feel half bad   when he calls me

| E / / / | F#7 / / / |

And you might call it sad and you might call me mad

| A / (G#) / | F#m / / / | E / / / |

But I've got one   who calls me   dad *(back to opening riff)*

CHAPTER
– 20 –

SELLING THE COOL CAR FOR YOU

THIS WAS WRITTEN SOMETIME AROUND THE MAKING OF THE *PADDOCK* *BUDDY* AND *SPIN! SPIN! SPIN!* RECORDS. I REMEMBER BECAUSE THE PARTICULAR CONVERSATION THAT INSPIRED IT WAS WITH CRAIG PILKINGTON, WHO ONE DRUNKEN EVENING IN THE STUDIO TOLD US OF HAVING TO SELL HIS BELOVED OLDSMOBILE WHEN HIS LIFE STARTED CHANGING, AND ALTHOUGH HE WASN'T EXPLICIT ABOUT THE EXACT SALE OF THE CAR, AND ALTHOUGH THE CAR IN THE SONG IS A DIFFERENT MAKE, IT'S PRETTY MUCH ALL THERE FROM HIS STORY. THE RETRO GIRL AND RETRO GUY TAG THAT COMES IN AT THE END WAS ACTUALLY ANOTHER SONG I WAS WORKING ON AT THE TIME — TOTALLY OBSERVATIONAL AND NOT PARTICULAR TO ME OR ANYONE ELSE.

Strangely enough, the phenomenon in the song was almost the reverse in my own personal case. When I met my wife Jenny she drove a reasonably neat EJ Holden. In fact, to quite a few people I knew around Northcote at the time she was known as 'the girl in the red EJ'. It was actually the standard Holden burgundy colour, but I think red just sounded better to everyone. When we started going out together I didn't own a vehicle at all, so hers was pretty convenient. After a period with neither, I now had a girl and a hip car, so that was a double win.

But the EJ Holden was manufactured in 1962 and this was 1997, so with a car that's already thirty-five years old you have to be careful how you treat it. I think I probably wasn't quite the person to be in charge of such a vehicle.

It was on a trip across town to get some recording gear serviced that I went over a bump, and I heard something spring loose underneath. It was just a small bracket holding the exhaust down near the boot of the car, and I thought nothing of it. Hell, this was an old vehicle — there's meant to be some rattling and scraping. But as it rattled and rattled and scraped and scraped, finally the larger bracket that held the muffler in place broke off, leaving the whole exhaust unit kind of floating — not to mention hitting the ground when I went over speed humps. Undeterred, I kept driving the beast, until the exhaust began to pull away from the motor (getting very loud now), finally ripping the carburettor off the side of the engine, meaning it couldn't deliver the fuel to make the car go. So the vehicle (inexplicably to me) just stopped.

Old cars. It's just old cars, I reasoned at the time.

And so, from what should have been a minor repair we now had a major repair on our hands, and not a lot in the way of cash to get it done. Someone made her an offer for the whole car, and before we knew it the red EJ was gone. You might have thought that would be the end of it, but sometime in the next month Jenny came in with the *Trading Post*, saying there was an EJ going cheap. Even

though it was a far less attractive khaki colour, before we knew it we were once again getting around town in another of Holden's finest from 1962.

The one thing I remember about this particular car — apart from the awful colour — was that the petrol gauge didn't work. I know this because on the very last Weddings tour we had a show at the Hallam Hotel on the outskirts of Melbourne. I took the green EJ out with Wally, who was living down the road in Northcote at the time. Later that night on the way home, somewhere coming into Clayton or Oakleigh, the old beast ran out of petrol, which I think we both knew at the time was a fitting metaphor for the band.

This was the writing on the wall for the green EJ. Jenny and I had now moved in together and we agreed running one vehicle was the prudent thing to do. With the Weddings gone, I was now in need of a vehicle that was serviceable enough to lug gear and get interstate occasionally — a workhorse. On the strength of yet another ad in the *Trading Post*,

one rainy afternoon a couple of guys drove up from the Latrobe Valley and in a quick transaction on the nature strip some money was counted out, some papers were signed, and the EJ was no longer ours. Or hers.

She'd sold the cool car. For me.

Even though the album *Spin! Spin! Spin!* began life with Al Barden behind the kit, Michael Barclay was the drummer on this recording. Craig played guitar and Rory played bass.

Preceding page left: Craig Pilkington. Photo: Mark Hopper

Preceding page right: The Sure Thing in Northcote. From left: Pilkington, Mick, Al Barden and Stu Speed. This is the Paddock Buddy line-up so probably around 2007

Opposite: The green EJ. Not the red one. The green one

Above: Mick driving one of a series of HiAces

M. THOMAS

SELLING THE COOL CAR FOR YOU

MUSHROOM MUSIC

(capo 2nd fret)

(riff)
| C / / / | / / / / | Am / / / | / / / / | G / / / | / / / / | F / / / | / / / / |

(verse)
| C / / / | C / / / | G / / / | G / / / |
As I change the midnight oil the household's fast

| F / / / | F / / / | Fm / / / | Fm / / / |
Asleep it's too late to change my mind there is a promise I must

| C / / / | C / / / | G / / / | G / / / |
keep what will they take in the morning half my life a set of keys

| Am / / / | Am / / / | F / / / | F / / / | C / / / | C / / / | Am / / / |
As they're kicking at the tires oh I'll bet that they'll look pleased

| Am / / / | G / / / | G / / / | F / / / | F / / / |
As the taillights pull away there's one more thing I have to say

(Chorus)
| Am / / / | G / / / | F / / / | F / / / |
I'm selling the cool car for you

| C / / / | B / / / | F / / / | / / / / |
I'm selling the cool car for you (It's a thing I gotta do)

(verse)
Once you've owned a car like that I guess there's no turning back
But I can't keep you by my side and keep a Buick on the track
It impressed you when we met it was all too plain to see
Now the point that you impress we need to get from A to B
As I watch the juniors train there's one more thing I have to say

SELLING THE COOL CAR FOR YOU

(chorus)

(mid)
Am / / / | Am / / / | Am / / / | Am / / / |
I'm not giving up my birthright   I'm not selling up the

E7 / / / | E7 / / / | F / / / | F / / / | *(back to the riff)*
farm there's more important things in life than getting a tan on my right arm

Do you ever get too old? Do you ever lose the need?
When it's all about the lines and it's not about the speed
And it's not that I'm unhappy the direction that we took
But sometimes I miss the faces of the people as they'd look
As their faces pull away there's one more thing I have to say

(double chorus)

(over the riff)
A retro girl and a retro guy in a big old Buick driving by
Retro car and retro kid retro does as retro did
A retro girl and a retro guy in a big old Buick driving by
Retro car and retro kid retro does as retro did

Limerick, Mid-West Ireland, 2001.

I'd done a couple of months in totally solo mode, and this can take its toll as you start wondering just what the hell you're doing bumping around various European countries while your friends at home are getting on with their lives. It can so easily feel you're never having much in the way of substantial conversations or meaningful exchanges, until you find yourself standing on a railway platform wondering what would happen if you were to throw your guitar under the next express train thundering through to Berlin or Bristol.

It's times like these you start to get a creeping feeling that you're getting incrementally further and further from home — both geographically and figuratively. I quite possibly might have played in Asia on my way through, then Europe, then England, Scotland, and here I was seemingly marooned in Ireland, which is almost as far as you can get from Melbourne, really. Every step seemed to be taking me further from where I wanted to be.

Still, in solo mode it can be quite profitable, and I'd be lying if I said there wasn't a certain satisfaction to be gained from getting all those miles behind you. One of my main problems with Weddings, Parties, Anything towards the end was the inability of the band to travel overseas to open up new territories. Ultimately, the band had just become unwieldy and expensive on the road, and with that fresh in my mind I was committed to the solo life for a good few years.

It was at the end of the tour and I was in Dublin staying with the booking agent who had put together a run of dates for me. The last one had been cancelled for some reason, so I had a couple of days to get through before my flight home. It was pleasant enough; he had a nice apartment on the (auld) canal and we actually managed to have the odd meaningful conversation. But the fact of it was that if I'd been allowed to bring my return flight to Australia forward I would have done it, so I was painfully aware I was simply killing time until the trip home.

On the third morning he came out and said he'd had a call and there was a show going in the town of Limerick that night, opening for an American woman — I have totally forgotten her name. He offered to pay my bus fare and I think the fee was 50 IEP (Irish Punt), which puts the tour somewhere around 2001 or 2002, as they stopped using that currency in 2002. It wasn't much of an offer, but rather than hang around Dublin drinking myself into oblivion I thought I may as well head west where at least, seeing as I now had a gig, I'd probably have someone else paying for the drinks. The thing is, up until that moment all my thoughts had been focused on the trip home, which I had thought would be from Dublin. And now I was heading further west, further away, all miles that would have to be reclaimed and retraced.

So, all fine — I caught the bus (three hours in drizzling rain and fading light, so not much to see), played the show and hung around to watch the main act. It was an okay pub; quite large and multi-purpose, with a big room for the main show, one for the inevitable traditional session, and plenty of places to sit and have a quiet drink. After a number of pints in the various bars, with various people, after I'd been asked where I was staying for the fifth time it began to dawn on me that I hadn't actually organised any accommodation. It'd been a long tour; months of flights, buses, trains, gigs, hotels, B&Bs and general things-to-be-organised. Weariness had set in and I'd just blocked the whole thing out. All I knew was that I would be getting on the plane home the next night, so my 6am departure from the Limerick bus station was about the only thing lodged in my brain.

Eventually there was a friend of the Dublin booking agent (quite possibly the promoter of the pub) who offered his couch, for which I was more than grateful. And of course we sat up drinking whisky, which always seems like a good idea, but never is. He eventually went to bed and threw some sort of blanket over me where I lay. At some stage of the night as I tried to locate the toilet I was confronted by the man's partner, who unleashed a virulent tongue-lashing, which was by this stage totally ineffectual. I really do recall it being a perfect maelstrom of verbal abuse, to which I wisely decided not to reply. Maybe I couldn't actually form the words. I don't think she was pretending to be scary. I was scared.

Looking back now, the bollocking I received was quite possibly the thing that stopped me getting too comfortable and sleeping through my wake-up call. Somehow I managed to drag myself up at 5.30am, as there was no way I wanted to be in the northern hemisphere an hour longer than I needed.

As I cheerfully packed up my things to head to the bus station for a three-hour trip to Dublin, a one-hour flight to Heathrow, then thirteen hours in the air to Singapore, then another ten to Melbourne, my previous night's drinking companion came out and asked what I was looking so damned happy about. (Obviously he'd found himself on the end of a similar flaming from the Old Lady.) I thanked him for the use of his couch, and told him simply that it was my first step in a homeward direction.

'Can I Sleep on Your Floor?' was recorded and produced by Craig Pilkington, who played guitar along with Rory Boast, who was on upright bass, and Michael Barclay on drums. I recall the key change in the song being a contentious issue during the recording, and I'm pretty sure it was Rory who insisted it was a single semi-tone from the original key, meaning a nice comfortable G suddenly becomes an A Flat, which is a pig of a key for a guitarist to perform a solo. Pragmatically, Craig just chose to become quick as lightning with his capo as a way of getting around the problem.

Preceding page left: Mick in a bottle shop up to no good. Amsterdam, 1998

Preceding page right: Outside Attila the Stockbroker's house (Attila in the doorway). Southwick, England, 2000

Following page: Riding to the gig. Amsterdam, 1998

CAN I SLEEP ON YOUR FLOOR?

M. THOMAS   MUSHROOM MUSIC

(verse)

E7 / A / | D →   G / / / | D / / / |
Can I sleep on your floor? I won't overstay my welcome

G / / / | D / / / | A / / / | A7 / / / |
I've just got the one show in your town

D / / / | D / / / | G / / / | D / / / |
But it don't pay so well   I cannot afford a hotel

G / / / | D / / / | A / / / | D / / / |
But there's no way I would want to let nobody   down You could

G / / / | D / / / | G / / / | D / / / |
think of it just as playing your part You'd be a patron of the arts

G / / / | D / / / | E7 / / / | A / / / | A / / /
And if you do this thing for me I'll write your name on my next CD

(E7 / / / | A / / / | E7 / / / | A / / / |
My video and my DVD I'm gunna write it all over my next CD)

(verse)
Can I sleep on that big old sofa? Really does look so inviting
I could put my guitar over there
And when the show is done and dusted we'll discuss all kinds of topics
Everything except the songs which no-one came to hear
But hey I bounce back pretty quick don't you get me wrong
A couple of drinks and a good night's sleep and I'll be back on song

(verse)
Let's get that air bed pump it pump it really now that's just the ticket
Don't tell me the damn thing's sprung a leak
But even if it has (pump it pump it) maybe that's not such a problem
It's the only thing gone down on me these past three weeks
And when your family's up to go to work here's what to say
That the shell of a man on the loungeroom floor will soon be on his way

Can I sleep on your floor? I won't overstay my welcome
I've just got the one show got the one show in your town
Hey I'm playing in your town

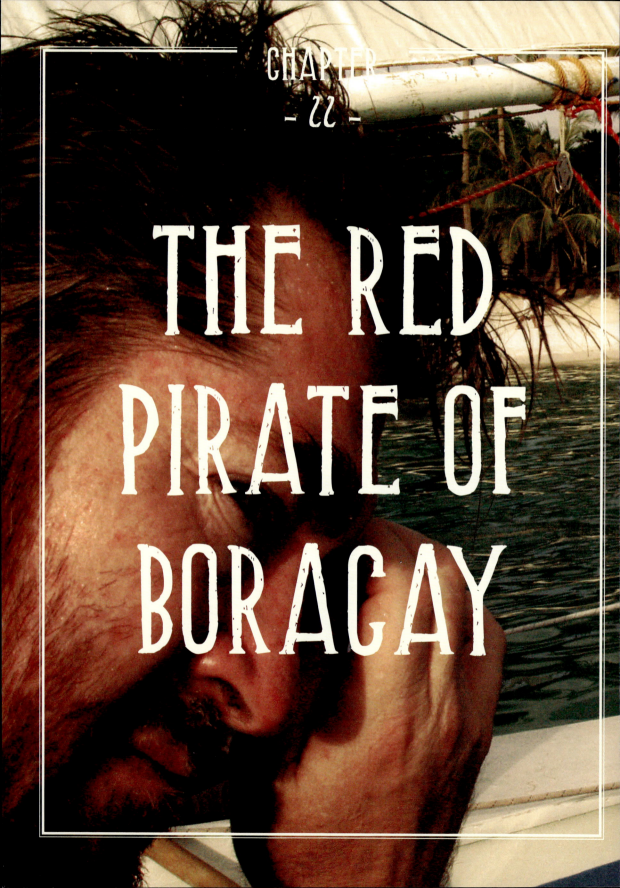

CHAPTER
- 22 -

THE RED PIRATE OF BORACAY

This is certainly the most unlikely song of the whole collection to have found its way onto a 'best of' compilation, and into this book. I feel that its merit lies in its conception as an organic piece of art that grew out of one thing that became another, and then resulted in something else entirely. 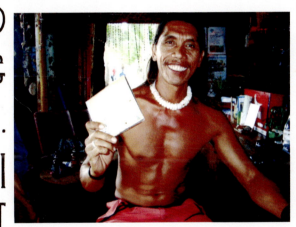 The other thing I enjoy is that it's a piece of work created in conjunction with a number of people who I have particularly enjoyed working with over the years, and so in some ways it tells a story in a creative, mechanical sense.

There was a song on *Dead Set Certainty*, my very first post-WPA album, called 'Big Geographical'. It concerned a friend's relationship with a girl who seemed to constantly solve her problems by relocating — doing a 'Big Geographical', as we called it. The north-west, Darwin, Perth, Sydney, central Australia, southern Tasmania — all these far-flung corners of Australia seemed to be her province and her refuge. It was a simple enough tune that was written while Weddings, Parties, Anything was still in existence, one we might've had a stab at if we'd stayed together, meaning it was part of the cache I had on hand once the band had finished. The Sure Thing Mark I recorded it in my backyard studio, and it went down to (ADAT) tape without incident. Perhaps the recording of those songs was a little low-key, but that tune never seemed to catch on much with anyone — musicians or punters. And I suppose experience tells me that sometimes you have to let them go.

When Michael Barclay suggested we have another shot at it for the album *Spin! Spin! Spin!* I was keen to see if we could make it come alive. He had the idea of changing the time signature in the middle part of the tune and making it illustrative of a journey in itself, like an aural travelogue. And then I took it one step further by having the song deconstruct totally, with just a faint echo of a sea-shanty version of the original tune. We hadn't played much with Squeezebox Wally for a while, so it was nice to have a reason to get him up to the studio to really underline the concept of the tune being a nautical journey in some ways. Very filmic and exotic, I thought at the time.

Spin! Spin! Spin! began life as a bunch of outtakes from the Paddock Buddy sessions that was recorded at the house we had for a number of years in Bealiba. I think when we'd originally set up we'd found ourselves pretty relaxed, and after going to all that trouble to set up a fully functioning studio it would have seemed a shame to stop working after a dozen songs had been recorded, so for that week we'd just kept trying different things. By the end of it we had over twenty band tracks, so there was plenty of stuff to form the foundation of a second album. And so it went that years after *Paddock Buddy* was released we began cutting and chopping, calling in favours for duets and writing the odd new bit here and there. It's an interesting way to work, and while not really typical for me it's in this context the convoluted origin of 'The Red Pirate' sits perfectly.

We realised during the mixing of *Spin! Spin! Spin!* that the actual tune Wally had played on 'Big Geographical' was only apparent as a faint echo, and that if it wasn't used in a more deliberate, purposeful form then it would be forever lost. And so there I was after setting out to rescue one tune from obscurity, trying to reconstruct and rescue another!

Around that time one of the records we had really been enjoying was the Aerial Maps album *Into the Blinding Sunlight* (in particular the track 'On the Punt'). Craig Pilkington, who was the guitarist with The Sure Thing as well as being the co-producer and engineer in the studio, was also an admirer of the spoken-word music mashup that the Aerial Maps and Adam Gibson had been creating, so he agreed Adam was a logical person to approach to see if he could come up with something for our now-orphaned accordion tune.

The other thing that happened around that time was the first Weddings, Parties, Anything reunion tour, which we decided to finish up in London. Squeezebox Wally pulled me aside and asked if there was anywhere in Asia I felt like stopping on the way back as some sort of celebration for the two of us surviving thirty years on the road together. I thought it was a good idea, and after a few enquiries we ended up heading to Boracay in the Philippines.

After the rigours of the last show celebrations in London, the surprise engagement party for Jen Anderson and merch-person Dave Suttie in Reading, then the flight to Manila and subsequent Cebu Airlines flight and creaky old boat to the island of Boracay, we found ourselves sitting at a beachfront restaurant, drinking beer and eating lobster and feeling for once that rock'n'roll wasn't too bad a profession for a couple of ageing gents to have spent their lives pursuing. It was a great week and a great way to celebrate. And it was there we lucked upon a strange and wonderful little bar called The Red Pirate. From memory it was carved out of driftwood, almost on the sand itself, and it was here I got to thinking about cultural exiles. I wondered if that mightn't be the perfect subject matter for Adam Gibson to tackle for this musical hybrid we had cooking away back in Craig's studio.

And so when I made it home I emailed the tune to Adam and had the briefest of conversations about the sort of people you run into in places like this … and he came up with the rest. The Floating Stone, the girl from Eastern Europe and the guy from South Australia, drinks with Neil Davis at the Caravelle — they're all his invention. But sit at a bar like The Red Pirate and it's all totally believable — and that's how the song came about.

Simple, really.

Preceding page left: Coming home from the final show of the 2008 reunion tour in London. Yes, eating lobster and yes drinking San Miguel. Philippines, 2008

Preceding page right: The actual Red Pirate himself. What a bar!

Following page: Adam Gibson and the Ark-Ark Birds at Woody's Bar, Collingwood. Melbourne, 2016. Photo: Mark Hopper

THE RED PIRATE OF BORACAY

M. THOMAS

LYRICS BY A. GIBSON

He came from South Australia she was from Eastern Europe
And they met in south-east Asia
And often that'll do it
Sometimes you've come so far that you can't go back again
Sometimes you've come so far that you can't go back again

Yeah the story went it was '75 he'd said so long Saigon
Got out in the second-last airlift
Memories of the Caravelle drinks with Neil Davis
Those beers they had before he was famous
And a pesky lawyer calling in from Melbourne
Asking about some money owed to someone somewhere somehow

Yeah so he'd said south China see you later
Went over to Nias Indonesia
Surfed the wave in its prime
Then across Sumatra dodging Suharto
Thought his tricks were definitely up this time
Thoughts his game was definitely up this time

So he washed up in Boracay on a boat called the Floating Stone
Flower blooms and unmade rooms
He was a good eleven-and-a-half years from home
A good eleven-and-a-half years from home
And there among the faded signs and the suntan lines
The lost hippies from the Apennines
He took up residence in the Red Pirate Bar
Sometimes you've come so far that you can't go back again
Sometimes you've come so far that you can't go back again

She had cheekbones that would make any man immediately change his plan
With a face like that in the Philippine night you'd never know where you stand
You'd never know where you stand
She was earning US dollars in a job she didn't care to define
While he propped at the bar of the Pirate and he waited for a sign
He waited for a signal a nod of any note
It's not the heat it's the humidity
It's not the heat it's the humidity
That'll bring undone any bloke

He came from South Australia she was from Eastern Europe and they met in south-east Asia
And often that'll do it
Sometimes you've come so far that you can't go back again
Sometimes you've come so far that you can't go back again

CHAPTER 23

SCORN OF THE WOMEN

Recently, someone sent me a link to a YouTube clip of 'Scorn of the Women' performed by a choir and instrumental ensemble from Scotch College in Melbourne. I was absolutely moved by the quality of the arrangement and the proficiency of the playing. My songs haven't had that many cover versions over the years and consequently this one had a real effect on me. I think there's something so considered and thoughtful in the instrumentation that makes this a really powerful rendition — I can hear the work that has been put into it. I thank John Ferguson, the director of music there, or whoever put the arrangement together.

But of course, the internet being the internet, and in particular Facebook being a place where people can have their say, I was quickly alerted to a discussion (argument?) going on regarding the merits of the song being performed in the hallowed halls of an institution such as Scotch College. While I am all for robust debate I think it's the words of Drizabone Dion Dickinson from Sydney's Handsome Young Strangers that appeared on the Weddings, Parties, Anything Appreciation Society page that finally, eloquently put the issue into perspective:

Yes, it's not a 'working class' version of the song but it's a cracking version nonetheless. Great arrangement. The instruments shine, sliding layers with each verse/chorus and love the mood the music sets in the softer 'takes more than bullets' verse.

Even if you feel the singers don't 'get' what they're singing (which is impossible to tell as they're a choir and need to pronounce words in the form of noted syllables) the arranger certainly understands the emotions of the song. 'Scorn of the Women' holds a special significance to me as it brought my mother-in-law to tears when she first heard it, and relayed her own story about how her dad received the white feather.

Such a haunting song from a great storyteller. It deserves to be considered folklore and this clip helps cement that status.

It's amazing what a compliment something like this is for a writer. I think the vast majority of totally positive comments the clip received reflect this, in that a lot of people who support an artist over a period of time need the same reinforcement in terms of their aesthetic decision. I smiled for days after hearing this version — as I said, I haven't had that many covers over the years.

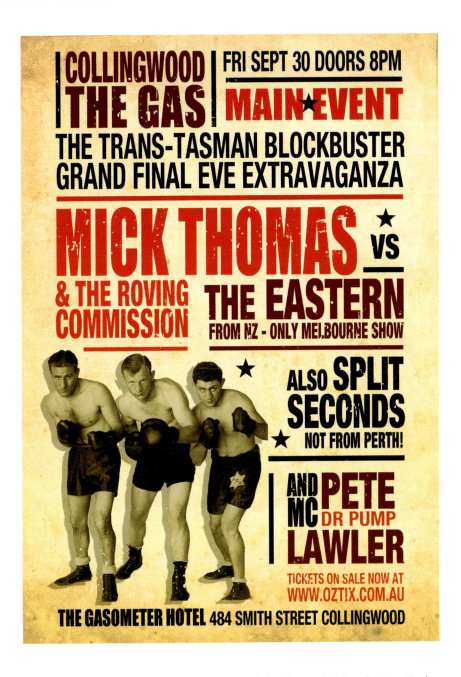

Preceding page left: Mick playing one of the 'Fraser Island' gigs. Melbourne, 2011

Preceding page right: Scotch College choir and ensemble. Melbourne, 2016

Opposite: Shelley Short and Mick at the Yarra Hotel. Melbourne, 2014. Photo: Mark Hopper

Above: Poster for Mick Thomas and the Roving Commission gig, 2016. Design: Jen Huntley

SCORN OF THE WOMEN

M. THOMAS
MUSHROOM MUSIC

(intro)
| G / / | D / / | Bm / / | A / / |
| G / / | D / / | Bm / / | A / / |

(verse)
| G / / | A / / | D / / | Bm / / |
Well I remember respectfully   like others before me   all

| Em / / | G / / | A / / | A / / |
those folk who fell in the   war   And

| G / / | A / / | D / / | Bm / / |
I heard you singing   songs of   lamentation   but I

| Em / / | A / / | D / / | D / / |
don't wish to   hear them   no more   And

| Em / / | G / / | A / / | A / / |
what did you   do in the   time of the war   is a

| Em / / | Em / / | A / / | A / / |
question asked   by   everyone   Well I

| G / / | A / / | D / / | Bm / / |
stood in the   line my   screwdriver in hand   making

| Em / / | A / / | D / / | D / / |
aircraft out   at   Laverton

(alternate line at the end of the third verse)
(Em / / | G / / | A / / | D / / |
… more than one way you   can   cripple a   man)

SCORN OF THE WOMEN

(chorus)

| G / / | G / / | D / / | D / / |
So don't sing no songs about Waltzing Matilda Don't

| A / / | G / / | A / / | G / / |
tell me I tried don't tell me I failed 'Cause

| G / / | G / / | D / / | Bm / / |
all I recall is the scorn of the women and a

| Em / / | G / / | A / / | G / / |
white feather that I received in the mail

(verse)
Well I remember the day I went down to enlist
And they said Read this chart on the wall
And I remember the tone of the voice of the doctor
As he said to me That will be all
And riding home slowly I sat on my tram
Not sure if to laugh or to cry
For to train in the camps a man needs his lamps
And a good soldier must have good eyes

(chorus)

(verse)
Well it takes more than bullets to murder to maim
Whether worn down or beaten a death's still a death
And you know sometimes when I think back to the forties
I pray for my very last breath
And you know I have nothing against those who fought
But for Christ's sake we do what we can
There's more than one way that you can skin a cat
And there's more than one way you can cripple a man

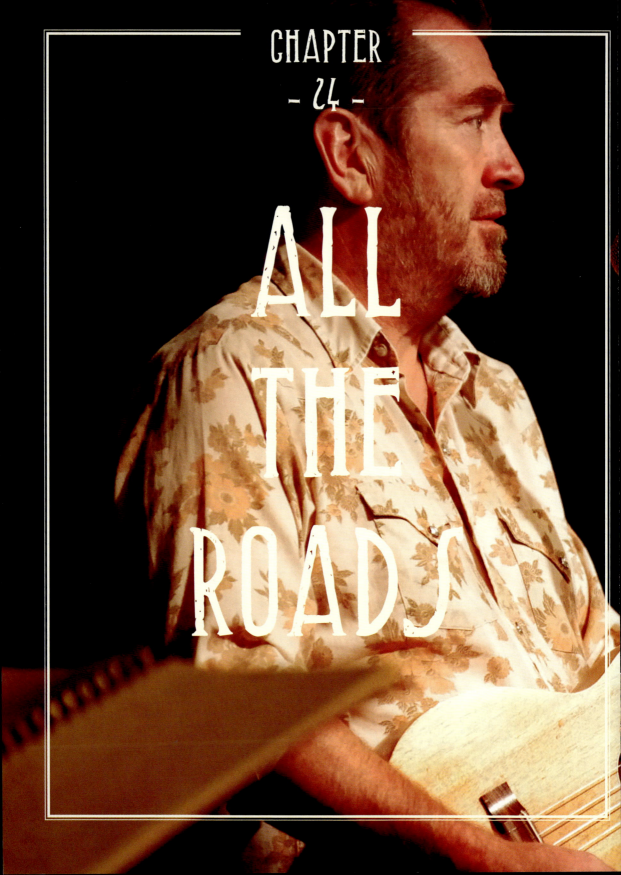

It's amazing how long an idea can hang around, and the way in which it can date a piece of music.

A song such as 'All The Roads' has a whole list of forensic signals linking it to various times in my life. I think at best songwriting is a hit-and-miss art form, and I've never been too good at carrying a notebook or keeping track of potential ideas, quotes and hook lines. I've always felt the really strong ones keep coming back around of their own accord, and at the most productive periods of my writing life my head has been a jumble of all these — both consciously and unconsciously. As I mentioned in the opening story of this book, I think this is the reason some songs just seem to 'fall out' in ten-minute spasms of creativity — in my opinion they're already half-written somewhere in the back of your mind. At best I might be able to find a date scrawled on a Spirex notebook somewhere, indicating the first draft of a tune. But often that's all I know about the song's creation.

Before I left Geelong in 1982, in the Never Never Band days, I remember I had a song containing the line 'all the lights were green for me'. I'm not sure the song even became a regular inclusion in our set, but I must have liked the idea in principle if it was to form the basis of another fully-fledged song over thirty years later.

The next line in the song that betrays an antiquated timeline is the one referring to 'coming home against the flow'. I attribute this directly to a conversation I had with a guitarist whose name I've long forgotten. He was playing with Jenny Morris, who the Weddings were opening for at a venue in Adelaide way back when we first hit the road. I'm pretty sure we were still a four-piece and I was still the bass player, as one thing that sticks in my mind was a small riser in the centre of the stage that the audience couldn't really see, but I recall people commenting it made me look like a giant with the big bass strapped around my neck. So if I was still on the bass then, I'd say we're talking around 1986.

The thing was, I had a nice conversation with this bloke (whose sister was apparently a fan of the Weddings) about the merits of what we were doing personally and creatively, and the financial and personal sacrifice it entailed. It was a really strong, mentoring-type exchange that must have had an effect, as I have a strong memory of him pointing out that as a professional musician you often find yourself driving against the flow of traffic. Driving into cities as everybody else drives out. Arriving as everybody else is leaving.

I guess it stuck with me, and every time we've found ourselves stuck in the van doing an overnighter it's a conversation I recall, and an ideal I take some little comfort in. But really, overnighters still stink, no matter how good the freeways are at that time of the day or night, no matter where you are planning on ending up, or how self-satisfied you are in your brilliant career.

The next line giving away a time and place is 'signs written there in blue', a reference to the bright blue signs of Melbourne's CityLink toll-road system. I've never been a great fan of bull-in-a-china-shop Victorian premier Jeff Kennett, the man that put them there, but I have to admit the roads are at the very least

'clearly marked in blue'. And I'd be lying if I denied it was also a direct reference to Bob Dylan's 'Tangled Up in Blue' — a favourite song of mine since its release in 1975. So Jeff's signs date the line in the song to sometime after the mid-nineties.

Lastly, the opening verse lists the generic freeways of any given Australian city — the East, the Western, the Ring Road, the Tunnel. I have a strong memory of a rowdy exchange in the tour van after a show in North America, as Pete Lawler bemoaned the unexciting nomenclature of Australian highways. Where, he passionately railed, was the Trans Canada of Gene Pitney? The Route 66 of Chuck Berry? The Ventura Highway of America? Or — most significantly — the A13 of Billy Bragg? I think this means the rant took place after an actual Billy Bragg show, meaning the thought was taking root in my psyche somewhere in the early nineties (probably on the Trans Canada between Montreal and Otawa, actually). I recall thinking it was a funny rave, though not entirely accurate as Australia does have some evocatively named roads. In light of this it was also possibly responsible for the playout of 'Driving Rain' from *Spin! Spin! Spin!*

And so with all these thoughts linking the origin of a song such as this to a plethora of incidents over the last thirty years, it's no wonder I appeared so vexed at a rehearsal recently when new Roving Commission person Ayleen O'Hanlon asked the simple question, 'When did you write that one?'

The recorded version features Darren Hanlon on bass, Squeezebox Wally on keys and accordion, and Adam Selzer on drums. Adam also engineered the session at Type Foundry Studios in Portland, Oregon.

Preceding page left: From JVG Brown River Show at Fitzroy Bowls Club. Melbourne, 2015. Photo: Mark Hopper

Preceding page right: The band (more or less) that made 'The Last of the Tourists'. From left: Adam Selzer, Darren Hanlon, Mick, Wally, Shelley Short and Alia Farah. Portland, Oregon 2012

Opposite: Mick in a Tarago just outside Beulah en route to Adelaide, 2014

Above: Mick Thomas and The Sure Thing. From left: Al Barden, Craig Pilkington, Stu Speed and Mick in Northcote. Melbourne, 2007

M. THOMAS — **ALL THE ROADS** — MUSHROOM MUSIC

(capo 2nd fret)

(intro)
```
G / / / | D / / / | A / / / | Bm / / / |
G / / / | D / / / | A / / / | A  / / / |
G / / / | D / / / | A / / / | Bm / / / |
G / / / | D / / / | A / / / | A  / / / |
D / / / | Bm/ / / | D / / / | Em / / / | D / / / | G / / / | D / / / |
```

(verse)

Bm / / / | A / / / | G / / / | D / / / |
The East The East it flowed like yeast the Western was a   sluggish beast The

Em / / / | Em / / / | G / / / | G / / / |
Ring Road was a   carpark stretching   twenty kilometres

Bm / / / | A / / / | G / / / | D / / / |
Tunnel closed conditions changed   a truck broke down on the inside lane The

Em / / / | Em / / / | G / / / | G / / / |
god of traffic   frowned I thought if   I can't join 'em   beat 'em

F#m / / / | F#m / / / | G / / / | G / / / |
But if the lights were green for me and every lane was   clean for me

Bm / / / | Bm / / / | A / / / | A / / / |
Coming home   against the flow   you'd know it was true

ALL THE ROADS

                                            (chorus)

        G / / / |D / / / | A / / / |Bm / / / |
All the roads   winding   all the ties   binding   Every

        G / / / |D / / / | A / / / | A / / / |
way   somehow getting   through   All the

        G / / / |D / / / | A / / / | Bm / / / |
wheels   turning and my   heart   churning   Every

        G / / / |D / / / | A / / / | Bm / A / |
sign   written there in   blue taking me   right back home to
*   (Every path clearly marked in blue)*

                                            (riff)
      D / / / | Bm / / / | D / / / | Em / / /| D / / / | G / / / | D / / / |
you

              When peak hour lasts for half the day
              And 'round it you can't find a way
              These roads they seem to make no sense
              These tolls they have no recompense
              Our lives are like this city map
              We narrowly avoid mishap
              To find our way back home again
              On highways lined with grief and pain
              But if the lights were green for you
              And every lane was clean for you
              As you came home against the flow well you'd know it was true

                              (chorus x 2)

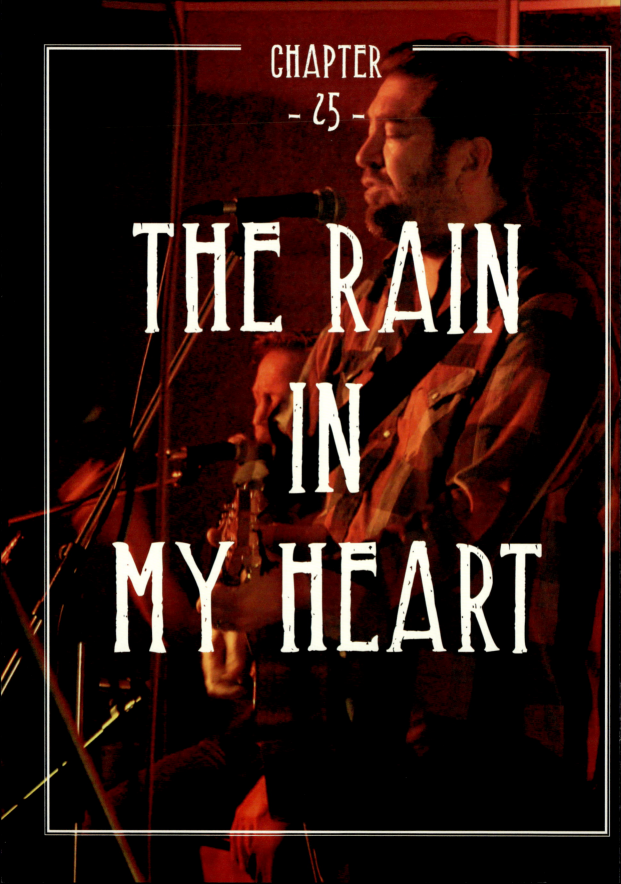

I HAVE SPENT A REASONABLE AMOUNT OF TIME IN THESE STORIES DEFENDING PEOPLE'S RIGHTS TO INTERPRET A SONG HOWEVER THEY CHOOSE. BUT SOMETIMES PEOPLE CAN GET THINGS SO HORRIBLY WRONG YOU JUST HAVE TO WONDER WHAT THE POINT OF PLAYING ACTUALLY IS. THROW IN A LANGUAGE BARRIER AND IT'S NOT HARD TO FIND YOURSELF TOTALLY QUESTIONING THE CULTURAL WORTH OF WHAT YOU DO.

The occasion that comes to mind was at the end of a tour in Europe. Myself and Michael Barclay had been really clocking up some serious miles on the autobahn, and were feeling pretty well-fried by the time the last of about fifteen straight shows came about. We had asked the tour promoter for some days off in the middle of the run, to which he had replied we were 'Australian pussies'. And as we weren't prepared to have our national character insulted we had taken on the challenge, and he had gone about filling every possible date of the three-week period with shows in towns we'd never heard of. It was fun, mildly lucrative, but exhausting.

The last of the run was in a little town outside Klagenfurt in the Austrian Alps. We had driven hours to get there, only to find we were billeted out with the family of one of the young promoters. It was a beautiful traditional Tyrolean-style farmhouse and we were in a shared room, the two beds not six inches apart. And Barclay snores. And I snore as well. We were just so tired that we lay down immediately to grab a few hours' sleep before sound check, only to be woken by the clanking of bells as the cows came in for the evening. We were in the back blocks. In retrospect it was a magical scene, although all we really cared about was sleep.

The show was in the basement of the town hall, and it was a wild affair from the start. This wasn't the cultured Austria of the Viennese. This was the mountains; this was more like the Balkans. These people were Slavic, proud and committed. There was little English spoken, and the drinking was fierce and unbridled. They were good-natured, but they were passionate about having a good time.

And so we played and played, they drank and drank. We ran out of songs. We played an encore, but it wasn't enough. We played another encore, but that wasn't enough. And then we decided we were finished, but they kept imploring us to do more. Even just *one* more. All right then, *one* more, but that was all.

The only song we had left was 'The Rain in My Heart'. As I muddled through the little faux Ink Spots guitar intro, they whooped with alcohol-induced recognition like we were playing the national anthem. They began stomping on the stage, and we responded by bashing the song out to get above the cacophony in a way it's just not supposed to go. And so they whooped even louder and sang along, even though they didn't know any of the words and didn't speak the language the song was being performed in, and all we could concentrate on was the drive to Munich and the flight home the next night. We had been away too long. The tour was over. We were done and 'The Rain in My Heart' would never be quite the same.

After the show they took us to a bar and fed us, and then to another bar where we (Barclay) could smoke and gave us more to drink, and then another where they hugged us and cried on our shoulders. For all I know they're still bashing out some sort of bastardised version of 'The Rain in My Heart' in the shadow of the mountains, while milking their beautiful storybook cows. Not falling apart — not much.

Preceding page left: Michael Barclay and Mick from a Valve Studios session that produced 'Head Full of Roadkill'. Solingen, Germany, 2009

Preceding page right: Mick and Barclay on stage, 2011

Above: Backstage at Mollongghip Hall with Sal Kimber and band

Following page: Poster for Mick and Barclay's 2010 European tour. Design: Jen Huntley

M. THOMAS

THE RAIN IN MY HEART

MUSHROOM MUSIC

(verse)
```
F  /  /  /  |Gm /  /  /  |C  /  /  /  |C  /  /  /  |
If you please   I've got nothing to say         That could

F  /  /  /  |Gm /  /  /  |C  /  /  /  |C  /  /  /  |
make this plain make your blues go away

Gm /  /  /  |C  /  /  /  |Gm /  /  |F  /  Gm /  |C  /  /  /  |C  /  /  /|
Time flies but  it don't heal   Can't hide   what anybody would feel
```

(chorus)
```
Gm  /  C  /  |F  /  /  /  |Gm  /  C  /  |F  /  /  /  |
I got the sun in my eyes I got the wind in my face I got the rain in my heart

Gm  /  C  /  |F  /  /  /  |Gm  /  /  /  |C  /  /  /  |
But I'm   falling in  line not falling   apart        oh oh oh
```

(verse)
Now the task at hand it's the life that we lead
It's the rent we pay it's the mouths that we feed
It's not wrong to cry
But it's wrong to weep while life passes by

(mid section over the chorus chords)
And out the back in the shed there's a surfboard
That we will not sell and nobody will ride
But let's leave it out there
Don't bring it inside oh oh oh oh

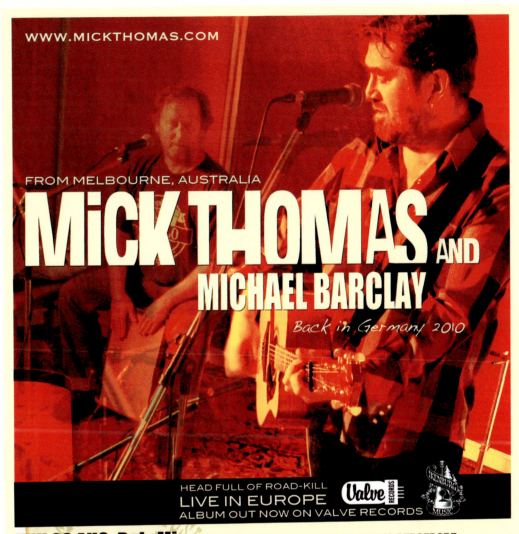

THU 26 AUG	BeLaMi	HOLTENKLINKER STR. 26, 21029 HAMBURG BERGEDORF
FRI 27 AUG	BERGWERK	QUELKHORNER LANDSTR. 19, 28870 QUELKHORN
SAT 28 AUG	ROCK AM MARKT	KIRCHENPLATZ 1 22848 NORDERSTEDT
SUN 29 AUG	WOODSTORE	GARTENSTRASSE 6, 31863 COPPENBRUEGGE
MON 30 AUG	KULTURBAHNHOF	BAHNHOFSTRASSE 22 49434 NEUENKIRCHEN-VOERDEN
TUE 31 AUG	SUBROSA	GNEISENAUSTR. 56, 44147 DORTMUND
WED 1 SEPT	GALERIE PESTPROJEKT	ALEXANDER-COPPEL-STR. 28, 42651 SOLINGEN
THU 2 SEPT	SUMPFBLUME	AM STOCKHOF 2A, 31785 HAMELN
FRI 3 SEPT	CAFE LIVE	HOLZENER STR. 31, 31061 ALFELD
SAT 4 SEPT	BRAUNER HIRSCH	BRAUNHIRSCHSTR. 21, 29223 CELLE

CHAPTER
– 26 –

THE LAST OF THE TOURISTS

Here's an article I wrote that appeared in *Great Ocean Quarterly* in January 2015

A PICTURE OF ANTALYA

Would you know what was relieved by the look on my face if you didn't know what had gotten me to that point? I doubt it very much. But when I look at that picture all these years later I am still filled with that same emotion. I am climbing an old wooden ladder out of the ocean onto some rocks. It was taken by my wife, looking straight down from above. The sun is shining, the water is a beautiful dappled blue-green and I am smiling

It was taken in Antalya, Southern Turkey, at a swimming spot off the rocks at the bottom of the Old Town where we were staying. Maybe I appear paler than usual. I had been sick, my wife had been sick. And we had been arguing. Fighting the way couples do on tour. What would the argument have been? Take your pick: Why didn't we stay in Greece? Why don't we go back to Greece? Why do we have to keep on moving? Why do we have to stay here? Why can't we stay here longer? Why did we pay that much for accommodation? Why don't we stay somewhere better? How is our money going to last? Why can't we lash out a bit? Why aren't we relaxing? Why are you so relaxed when I'm not relaxed? Am I the only one worrying about these things?

A few days earlier the bus trip from the east of the country had been a ghoulish overnight nightmare. The seats, threadbare and hard, gave little chance for sleep as a succession of awful videos screeched on a small television above the driver's head. It was alternately draughty and clammy, smelly and crowded to capacity. To make matters worse, in the middle of nowhere in the middle of the night I'd almost had us thrown off for swigging from a raki bottle. For all its apparent secular modernism Turkey can still observe some pretty basic tenets of the Muslim faith in things like public consumption of alcohol. So how cruel the main spirit available was the most pungent and easily detectable. Call us overly sensitive, but the fact that most of the other passengers on the bus suddenly seemed to hate us really did add to our overall discomfort.

We'd arrived in Istanbul in the early morning weary and confused, and walked the city for over an hour to find that the best room on offer was the one the first tout had recommended as we'd stepped from the bus. We'd finally secured this beautiful room overlooking the Golden Horn and then descended into a deep sleep — only to be awoken by the screeching of tannoy speakers right outside our window blaring the muezzin's afternoon call to prayer.

We'd spent some strangely peaceful days there prowling the mosques and bazaars, but ultimately decided to keep on moving, heading back south to the sun and the ocean. Always moving, having to extract every bit of experience from a limited timeframe. Moving, but not always experiencing or enjoying — or agreeing, for that matter.

I think I'd come seeking the Mediterranean of Lawrence Durrell, Henry Miller and Patrick Leigh Fermor. From a youth spent poring over the travel books of Gerald Durrell and Paul Theroux and the novels of Graeme Greene and Charmian Clift, I was left a thirst for the sort of authentic romantic experience that apparently flourishes in such places. And suddenly there we were, with the money from a couple of decent gigs in London stuffed in our bag and a month to spend it.

So, back to the photo and that morning on the ladder: Jenny had been sick, really sick, for almost a week. Earlier that month we'd taken a boat out of a southern port with some other couples (travelling with your partner, you always seem to end up with other couples). Once at sea Jenny had come down with basically stock-standard tourist-in-Turkey dysentery. The men running the boat were sure it was sea-sickness but they were wrong, and the sickness seemed to take hold, waning intermittently then returning with a vengeance every few days, never quite leaving her, never quite laying us up for too long. But by the time we made it to Antalya she was weakening to a point where she couldn't keep going. Of course, I wanted to keep checking destinations off the list, and maybe this was the origin of this particular conflict.

However, the argument had begun, we'd reached a point where I'd seen fit to leave her lying on the bed in a small pensione in the Old Town, and headed up to sit sullenly outside a restaurant looking out over the ocean. It was hot and still, and every time the waiter came over to serve me a beer he suggested I try a kebab — and every time I took a look at the layers of meat spindling in the direct sunlight I steadfastly shook my head and motioned to the beer as a standing order. The diesel fumes from the countless trans-Mediterranean ferries sat low over the ocean and a silent stillness seemed to envelope the promontory on which sat the old fort.

For some hours the turmoil of the past few days seemed to subside.

Ultimately, Jenny staggered up unsteadily from our abode, and after a few drinks the argument seemed to resume. Let's stay here, let's go somewhere better …

As we sat there in uncomfortable silence, staring out over the water, the ever-persistent waiter approached for the twentieth time asking if I was wanting a kebab. I guess it was pure bloody-mindedness, but at some point I suddenly relented and said of course, of course, of course — give me the kebab, the pink

Prededing page left: Mick on the rocks at Antalya, 2000

Preceding page right: Motorbiking somewhere in Turkey, 2000

Opposite: Mick having a swim near Antalya, 2000

sweating chicken kebab that has been sitting in the sunlight all day. Give it to me, give it to me now.

And Jenny said no, don't Mick, don't eat it, and I said Christ, it's the only way he'll ever leave me alone, and so twenty minutes later something had gone completely wrong internally, and well, there's nothing to bring a couple together like mutual bouts of dysentery. There was suddenly no dissention concerning when we would leave the town, where we could afford to stay, what we would eat — or ultimately when we would go and find a doctor. It was a matter of us working through it all together, and it would be a good while before we were able to even contemplate plans to resume our quest for the romantic Mediterranean.

For the next few days the one activity that seemed to make any sense to me was a quick swim first thing in the morning.

And that's when I discovered the old wooden ladder off the rocks a couple of hundred yards from where we were staying. Pretty soon a young entrepreneur had set up a makeshift bar on the rocks to sell me a couple of Efes Pilseners as my strength slowly returned day by day. The sunlight seemed a constant, as did the particular shade of aquamarine, and when Jenny was able to finally join me I knew that things were definitely mending and that in some spiritual way this was the tonic we required more than anything.

And so when I look at the photo what I see is the end of a week and the end of a conflict. I see the health and strength we found in the sunlight, in the bazaars and markets of Antalya's Old Town, in a weird backstreet bookshop (The Owl, as I recall) and in the ocean itself, that was always there and strangely enough hardly patronised by anyone other than us. So I suppose in some small way (dysentery aside) this was the Mediterranean I had read about and idealised.

And in that look on my face perhaps you'll discern my relief that maybe, for a brief moment, I'd discovered the literary ocean I had come to find.

Right: Original book jackets. From left: Mani *by Patrick Leigh Fermor,* Bitter Lemons *and* Prospero's Cell *by Lawrence Durrell*

Opposite: Mick climbing the ladder out of Mediterranean. Antalya, 2000

THE LAST OF THE TOURISTS

M. THOMAS
MUSHROOM MUSIC

(intro)
| Em / / / | Em / / / | Em / / / | Em / / / |
                                    When the

(a-verse)
| Em / / / | D / / / | Em / / / | Em / / / |
last of the   tourists had   gone   Well the

| Am / / / | Cmaj7 / / / | D / / / | D / / / |
town   felt stupid   Like a

| D / / / | D / / / | D / / / | D / / / |
fading paramour   abandoned and bereft   As the

| Em / / / | D / / / | Cmaj7 / / / | D / / / |
last of the   tourists   packed his bags and left and when the

| Em / / / | D / / / | Em / / / | Em / / / |
last of the   tourists was   gone

(a-verse)
And when the last of the tourists had gone
Well the town felt nervous
There was nobody left to sell to swindle or to cheat
Just a multitude of mopeds moping in the street
And when the last of the tourists had gone

(b-verse)
| D / / / | D / / / | D / / / | D / / / |
And like a henna tattoo the beauty of the town   Would

| Cmaj7 / / / | G / / / | D / / / | D / / / |
fade with the   season   Until the

| D / / / | D / / / | Cmaj7 / / / | Cmaj7 / / / |
beauty of the town with the   last of the tourists   had

| Em / / / | Em / / / | Em / / / | Em / / / |
gone

THE LAST OF THE TOURISTS

(a-verse)
And when the last of the tourists had gone
Well the town felt lonely
And the prices in the cafés they were all wrong
The band was in the tavern sick of all their songs
And when the last of the tourists had gone

(b-verse)
Like they'd sold off the summer
And sold the salt from the ocean
Now the sun in the sky
With the last of the tourists had gone

(a-verse)
And when the last of the tourists had gone
Well the town felt let down
And the waitress who'd been laid off she walked along the pier
And she dreamed of the one who'd gone and left her there
And when the last of the tourists had gone

(b-verse)
Was it the end of the world or the end of the season?
As she got on the bus you know it felt like treason
And the beauty of the town
With the last of the tourists the last of the tourists had gone

CHAPTER 27
TOMMY DIDN'T WANT YOU

LEAVING YOUR GUITAR IN THE BACK OF THE CAB — IT'S ONE WAY TO REALLY MESS UP THE MEMORY OF A GREAT TOUR OR SHOW. AND IT'S SO EASY TO DO. I'VE DONE I T HALF-A- DOZEN TIMES AND SOMEHOW ALWAYS MANAGED TO GET THE INSTRUMENT BACK. BUT, AS JENNY KEEPS TELLING ME, ONE DAY I WON'T BE SO LUCKY. I GUESS SHE'S RIGHT

The incident referred to in the last verse of 'Tommy Didn't Want You' took place around 1996, which was easy enough to work out as that was the year Jenny and I began seeing each other. She was working at Chick Ratten's Rainbow Hotel in Fitzroy, and it was her I'd impulsively jumped from the cab in Brunswick Street to go and meet.

It was a 'long week' the guitar stayed away from me, and when I was finally contacted by the cab driver he insisted I come to his house and sing Frank Sinatra's 'My Way' to earn the guitar back. He actually videoed the performance, and I've often meant to drop in and ask if I could have a look, but it's probably up on YouTube already now that I think of it. Regrets, I've had a few …

For the rest of the story the song tells it pretty much how it happened. The guitar in question was made under specification for Tommy Emmanuel, who decided he didn't like it after all, upon which the people at Maton Guitars thought it would be a good instrument for me — and so they offered me the guitar at a reduced rate. I enquired as to why it was so cheap, and when they finally told me I suddenly felt uncomfortable about the transaction. I drove away from the factory accompanied by the Wedding's stage guy Stan, who convinced me to turn around and drive back for the instrument.

In the most recent line-up of the Roving Commission, on bass guitar and lap steel we have had Michael Hubbard, who happened to work at the Maton guitar factory around the period in question. He says on the factory floor there really wasn't much talk at all about the incident (i.e. none), so I suppose the line 'all the boys in the factory knew' was stretching it a bit.

The guitar is confined to the studio these days; pretty much the pride of the fleet, as far as the guitars I have from the Maton factory. It's done its fair share of miles. The 'scars' referred to in the song have been nearly all incurred as a result of it sitting on stage night after night during the Weddings song 'Ticket in Tatts', when the stage was ritually showered with coins.

'Tommy Didn't Want You' was pretty much the closing tune of our live set for a long time, and I'll always think of it as a signature song for some of The Sure Thing's later line-ups. The recorded version featured Al Barden on drums, Rory Boast on upright bass and Craig Pilkington on guitar, with Chris Altmann guesting on pedal steel.

Preceding page left: On stage at Tamworth, 2009

Preceding page right: The band at Bealiba while recording Paddock Buddy. From left: Mick, Al Barden, Craig Pilkington and Rory Boast. This makes it around 2006

Opposite: Mark Hopper helped mock up this collage for the cover of the 'Aqua Profonda' single which came out 2015. It is more or less a direct copy of the first WPA EP from 1985. The Roving Commission in the picture from left: Michael Hubbard, Mick, Dave Folley and Wally

TOMMY DIDN'T WANT YOU

M. THOMAS
MUSHROOM MUSIC

(riff)
E / A / | D / A / | E / A / | D / A / |

(chorus)
E / A / | D / A / | E / D / | B / / / |
Tommy didn't want you   And I had second   thoughts it's true

E / A / | D / A / | E / D / | B / / / |
All the   boys in the   factory knew that   Tommy didn't want you

F#m / B / | E / A / | D / A / | E / A / |
Tommy didn't want you

D / A / |

(verse)
E / A / | D / A / | E / A / | D / A / |
Now what was I thinking I must've been blind anyone could see you were one of a kind

E / A / | D / A / | E / A / | D / A / |
Your body was small your neck was strong   the signs were there but I read them wrong

E / A / | D / A / | E / A / | D / A / |
(I said the signs were there I read them wrong the signs were there I read them wrong)

E / A / | D / A / | E / A / | D / A / |
'Cause I couldn't stand the thought of him holding you checking you out saying you won't do

E / A / | D / A / | E / A / | D / A / |
If you're made of wood your heart still breaks but what that guy wants that guy takes

TOMMY DIDN'T WANT YOU

(chorus)

(verse)
Now my mate Pat and my friend Stan
They told me that I shouldn't worry 'bout the man
But when I saw you smile from the floor that day
Well I got in my car and I drove away
(Yeah I got in my car and I drove away
I got in my car and I drove away)
But I was driving real slow talking you down
Good advice made me turn around
If it's nothing to him it's nothing to me
But I can see something that he can't see

(chorus)

(verse)
Well for ten years now you've stood by me
I sang the Four Corners sang the Seven Seas
Though you bear the scars of the miles we've done
It's never been easy it's always been fun
(It's never been easy it's always been fun
It's never been easy it's always been fun)
But when I left you in a cab down on Brunswick Street
For the longest week you stayed away from me
But I got you back it didn't seem wrong
Like the way that you came I got you for a song

(chorus)

(ending play out)

| E / A / | D / A / | F#m / B / |
Who cares what that guy thinks   Tommy didn't want you

| E / A / | D / A / | F#m / B / |
Who cares what that guy thinks   Tommy didn't want you

| E / A / | D / A / | F#m / B / |
Who cares what that guy thinks   Tommy didn't want you

E / A / | D / A / | E→

From left: Julian Chick, Nico O'Mara, Mick, Dave Folley and 'Squeezebox' Wally. Greendale Hotel, 2014. Photo: Mark Hopper

CHAPTER 28

THE CAP ME GRANDA' WORE

One time when Christie Moore played in Geelong, my brother Steve bought tickets for my parents and they went along. They didn't enjoy the show and both said they thought the music he played was 'morbid'. But I could've told my brother that was the way they judged Irish music generally. It was never their thing. I have distinct memories of my mother's disappointment when I veered from junior garage bands playing brassy rhythm-and-blues, and started experimenting with mandolins, accordions  and fiddle players. She was adamant her father (my granpa' — as opposed to the granda' in the title of the song) had hated that sort of music, and even went as far as to say she had been forbidden to go out with Irish boys when they had lived in Collingwood between the wars. 'Stay away from the Paddies,' was her advice.

So where does my affinity for Celtic music come from? The truth is I'm not entirely sure. It was there pretty early and developed of its own accord, as far as I can see. There was no iconic, irascible old Irishman who sat with me around a kitchen table as I came of age, no inspired performance or even film that I might have seen to influence me in this regard. But somehow, by the age of fifteen, I found myself hanging around the Geelong Folk Club, saving up for tickets to see the Chieftains at the Geelong Palais, or getting my parents to drive me to Melbourne for various folk gigs. As it said on the back of a Chieftains album I bought back then, it was 'music to give you memories you never had'. And to cap it all off, I was brought up Protestant!

But somewhere along the way I drifted from that music, moved to Melbourne and started playing in rock bands. I still had an ear for it generally, but I just thought perhaps Mum was right and it was never going to be my thing either. Then one night in 1982 when I was living on my own in Brunswick, driving cabs on weekends while I finished off my arts degree by correspondence ('off campus', we called it, as opposed to 'online'), I dropped someone at the Dan O'Connell Hotel in Carlton. I thought I saw Andy Irvine from Irish supergroup Planxty standing outside, talking to someone. As I picked up another fare I commented that the guy looked like Andy Irvine (from Irish supergroup Planxty) and the passenger confirmed that it was actually him — Andy Irvine from Irish supergroup Planxty! I asked what he was doing there, and they said he'd been playing in town somewhere or other and had come to the Dan 'for the craic'. He said it quite casually, as if it was something that happened all the time.

So the next night I thought I'd better go and investigate the Dan O'Connell and see what 'the craic' actually was. It all started opening up to me, and I began experiencing 'the memories I never had' once again. It was as clear as mud, or at least as Guinness, I suppose. And every few years there seemed to be something or someone to reconnect me with that music and that scene.

When the Weddings first went to Sydney, after our very first show opening for Stevie Ray Vaughan at the Hordern Pavillion (with an impressionable fifteen-year-old in the audience by the name of Tim Rogers, I was later to discover) we all adjourned to the White Horse Hotel in Surry Hills. Here, there happened to be a band called The Gingermen playing — with Pete Lawler on bass, no less. I'm not sure a lot of people realised that at the time he joined the Weddings, Pete came from a background of playing in Irish bands around Sydney. After he'd been in the band a few years the drift away happened again, but variously it would be halted by impromptu Irish sessions we lucked upon, records lent to us by passing strangers, relationships in general that would bring us back to 'the auld stuff', to 'the craic'.

And then Pete left the band, only to be replaced by Stephen O'Prey — 'Irish' O'Prey, as he has always been known. And even though his musical background with The Badloves was far more The Commitments than Christie Moore, it was obvious that when I wanted to write a song like 'The Cap me Granda' Wore', he'd be the perfect resource.

When the Weddings had begun, pubs like The Dan O'Connell in Melbourne or the White Horse in Sydney were Irish pubs by weight of their history as institutions, servicing areas with large immigrant Irish populations. The music that was a by-product of that kept their identities strong as the Celtic proportion of the surrounding areas dwindled. But by the early nineties it didn't seem to matter where you were (Dubai? Albury? Southbank? Bali?), there'd be some sort of Irish pub on hand and

a bored covers band playing 'Brown Eyed Girl' or 'Dirty Old Town'.

'The Cap Me Granda' Wore' is one song written well before the Weddings had decided to finish up. We played it on and off for a period, but as it was toward the band's end, getting new tunes on the set list was becoming murderously difficult. Stylistically, if it'd been on one of the earlier albums I think it could have become a pivotal song. It's always been a lot of fun to play, and barring the time I told a new drummer (Ryan James) that it should speed up 'as fast as he could play it', not taking into consideration he was a good deal younger than me, it's been a vital part of the machine having a real knees-up to put near the end of the set.

This was recorded for *The Horse's Prayer*, with Craig Pilkington on guitar, Stu Speed on bass and Michael Barclay on drums (plus Bruce Haymes on keys). I played all the mandolins and bazoukis, as we were content enough with the basic band to resist the temptation to enlist a great big Celtic melody section.

Preceding page left: Taken for the Vandemonian Lags project under a bridge in Abbotsford. Photo: Leigh Mackenzie

Preceding page right: Stephen O'Prey and Mick from the Age EG Hall of Fame induction of WPA in 2012

Above: Mick thinking about heading into The Victoria Hotel. Melbourne, 2005

M. THOMAS / S. O'PREY

THE CAP ME GRANDA' WORE

MUSHROOM MUSIC

(intro)
| Am / / / | C / G / |
| Am / / / | F / D / |

(Verse)
| Am / / / | C / G / |
Well who could blame me?   I was just a lad of   eighteen years

| Am / / / | F / D / |
Looking for adventure   I was heading for the sun

| Am / / / | C / G / |
I left the polytechnic   left it for the southern hemisphere

| Am / / / | F / / / |
Me ma said not to drink too much I knew that I'd drink far too much

| Dm / / / | G / / / |
'Cause Dezzy Riley wrote me and he told me it was so much fun

| Am / / / | F / / / |
The day that I got off the plane he met me there with Frank McShane

| Dm / / / | C / D / |
They took me to the city and we stopped in for the one and I saw a…

(chorus)
| G / / / | Am / / / |
Hurling stick from Derry   and a door knocker from Cork

| C / / / | F / C / |
A cap upon the wall just like the one I saw me granda' wearing

| G / / / | Am / / / |
Up above the doorway   De Valera smiling down   At a

| C / / / | D / G / G# |
poster in the hallway of the pubs of Dublin Town

(verse)
Well who could blame me? I could hold a tune and play a bit
I'd only ever been in rock bands but me accent it was right
So we played the tunes we sang the songs and I do believe I was a hit
And I liked the girl behind the bar she was out six months from Mulengar
We'd all stop and have a jar after work on Friday nights
She told me that she loved this place I lent across I kissed her face
Me Irish heartbeat it did race me Celtic head felt light
Beneath the…

(chorus)

(verse)
But who could blame me? I was now a man of nineteen years
It was the first time I'd spent Christmas on me own.
Me visa had expired I'd begun to like Australian beer
And the cap upon the wall just like the one I saw me granda' wearing
Made me long for Ireland and I booked me ticket home
I walked into the house in Dublin city asking of me family history
The photos and the trinkets and the cap me granda' owned
But then me ma she looked at me in shock she said me boy we sold the lot
To a pleasant man from Melbourne who called us on the phone
She'd sold the…

(extended chorus)
Hurling stick from Derry and a door knocker from Cork
The cap upon the wall it was the one I saw me granda' wearing
Up above the doorway De Valera had come down
And an ashtray that me da' stole from a pub in Dublin Town.

An accordeon from Italy that had never played a tune
A shamrock made of plastic and the world cup team from ninety
A horseshoe and a briar pipe an ancient brick of peat
I looked down in surprise to see the floor beneath my feet.

A recording by the Waterboys a recipe for stew
A litre of the Liffey and a picture of James Galway
The text books from the Poly over which we used to toil
And a paperback edition of the works of Roddy Doyle.

She'd sold the crystal vase from Waterford the cup from Donegal
She'd gone and sold the toilet seat I had to stand to do me business
A blackthorn stick from Arklow some driftwood from the shore
The fiddle in the attic and the sash me father wore.

She'd sold the hurling stick from Derry and a door knocker from Cork
The cap upon the wall it was the one I saw me granda' wearing
Up above the doorway De Valera had come down
And an ashtray that me Da' stole from a pub in Dublin Town
So I think perhaps I'll get drunk at the pub in Dublin Town

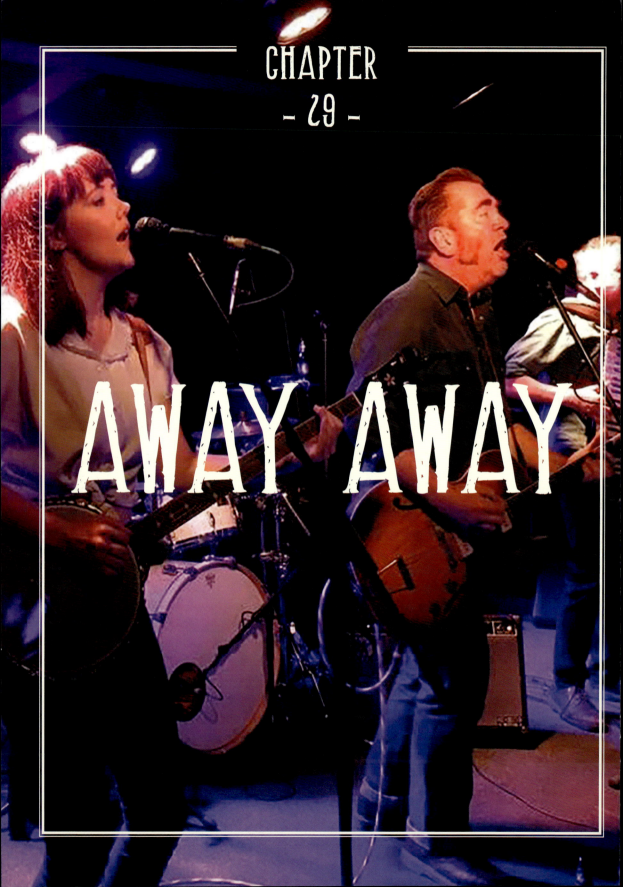

CHAPTER 62

AWAY AWAY

REMEMBER HAVING A STAB AT 'AWAY AWAY' WITH A FORMER BAND (PRE-WPA, I MEAN) AND IT NOT SOUNDING QUITE RIGHT IN RETROSPECT, THE OVERALL SOUND AND CONCEPT OF THAT BAND HAD BECOME CONVOLUTED AND CONFUSED. THE FACT I HAVE TROUBLE REMEMBERING WHAT THE BAND WAS EVEN CALLED IS SIGNIFICANT. IN THAT I THINK AT THIS POINT IN TIME I HAD ENDED UP A LONG WAY FROM WHERE I'D BEGUN. SOME FRIENDS WHO HAVE REMAINED CONSTANT SUPPORTERS OVER THE YEARS CAME TO A SHOW SOMEWHERE IN TOWN AND FINALLY HAD THE COURAGE TO TELL ME THEY THOUGHT IT JUST WASN'T WORKING AND THE WAY THIS SONG SOUNDED WAS THE PUREST INDICATION OF THE FACT. IT'S A TOUGH THING TO BE TOLD AND I'M NOT SURE HOW I TOOK THE NEWS AT THE TIME

Not long after that the drummer, who was the main collaborator in that band, came around to collect his kit from my house. He said he also thought we were going nowhere and he was wasting his time. If my friends had been concerned and sensitive in the way they had given their opinion, this was nothing like that. His judgement was aggressive and brutal. There was no mistaking my creative aspirations as a player had led me to a significant point. I was devastated by this apparent honesty. It took a while to know what to do.

I was in my early twenties and had begun my career as a writer wanting to play lyrical, melodic, modern folk rock music, and somehow had drifted from this ideal. I'd started in Geelong and eventually relocated to Melbourne, which felt like a mammoth upheaval. Each subsequent band and constantly changing line-up of under-rehearsed, non-committal players and totally inappropriate shows seemed to see me further and further from my initial concept. But suddenly I had this song that I could play to friends on an acoustic guitar that sounded fresh and inspiring — but just didn't work with the bands I had found myself playing with.

It was enough reason to stop playing entirely and go away to work on a bunch of new songs that would sit comfortably alongside this one — which was really how the Weddings and the next part of my career began. I've always felt that the concept of tenacity is overrated in the arts, and sometimes it's good to throw up your arms and just quit the whole thing. 'Away Away' was the catalyst for me to do just that.

So although it's easily our oldest song, it's quite possibly all this added significance that makes it the one we enjoy playing the most. As we play it now we are not that different to the people who look to our music purely as a trigger for memory, and therefore can hear all the different layers supplied by the various players over the years — Janine Hall's bass part that Michael Hubbard seems to have intuitively readopted via Stephen O'Prey and Pete Lawler, Barclay's double-time drum bit that he added when he joined the Weddings, which disappeared for a few years and was brought back by Dave Folley. Dave Steel's guitar riff, handed down through Jen Anderson, now played by Ayleen O'Hanlon on the banjo, the vocals Barclay sang in the studio before he was actually in the band. And Wally's accordion riff, that was pared back in the studio to a point where it was nearly lost for good but was reinstated.

And the singing of the audiences everywhere — often gloriously misplaced and impatient for the chorus bits that only officially happen a couple of times, but on a good big night seem to occur maybe a few more times than necessary.

It's been a more than useful tune. I remember one night at the Trade Union Club in Sydney, Janine Hall made me promise to never omit it from the set. Oh Janine, how right you were.

Preceding page left: Mick Thomas and the Roving Commission at the Gasometer. From left: Ayleen O'Hanlon, Mick and 'Squeezebox' Wally. Melbourne, 2016. Photo: Mark Hopper

Preceding page right: Mick and Janine Hall from the very first film clip WPA ever made. It was shot at the Missions to Seafarers on Flinders Street. Melbourne, circa 1987. Photo: Steve Thomas (Mick's brother)

Opposite: Poster for Mick Thomas and the Roving Commission album launch, 2013. Design: Jen Huntley

AWAY AWAY

M. THOMAS

MUSHROOM MUSIC

(riff)
| D / / / | D / / / | Em / / / | G / / / |
| D / / / | D / / / | Em / / / | G / / / |

(verse)
| D / / / | D / / / | Em / / / | G / / / |
A picture's worth a thousand words but it can   barely scratch the

| D / / / | D / / / | Em / / / | G / / / |
surface   Of all I have seen and heard and while all around is

| D / / / | D / / / | Em / / / | G / / / |
worthless   I see you in sepia   I see you in black and

| D / / / | D / / / | Em / / / | G / / / |
white   Even in my wildest dreams   even on my darkest

| A / / / | A / / / | G / / / | G / / / |
night can't leave it there can't let it drop can't walk away

| A / / / | A / / / | G / / / | G / / / |
I have you hanging on my wall   and I sing every single

(chorus)
| D / / / | Em / / / | G / / / | Em / / / |
day   Away away   where only   memory   can

| D / / / | Em / / / | G / / / | Em / / / |
find you   Away away   leaving   this poor fool behind

| D / / / | Em / / / | G / / / | Em / / / |
you It's just a memory   and though I can hardly

| D / / / | Em / / / | G / / / | Em / / / |
See   photos of better days   almost good enough for me

AWAY AWAY

(verse)
I wake up on restless days so much noise so little sleep
I just lie awake in bed I resolve to make believe
And imagine that you're here that you never went away
It gets so easy to dream it gets so hard to face the day
I can't forget I won't forget but honestly what can you do?
When I hate everyone I hate everything that's keeping me from you

(chorus)

(mid)
| D / / / | Em / / / | G / / / | A / / / |
Away away   away away   away away

| D / / / | Em / / / | G / / / | A / / / |
Away away   away away   away away

(playout)
| D / / / | Em / / / | G / / / | A / / / |
| D / / / | Em / / / | G / / / | A / / / |

CHAPTER
– 30 –

AUSTRALIAN FLAG BIKINI
(AFB)

AFTER A GREAT SHOW AT THE CARAVAN CLUB IN OAKLEIGH, I WAS AT THE MERCH STAND DOING THE BUSINESS AND SIGNING AS MUCH STUFF AS HUMANLY POSSIBLE. THERE WAS A YOUNG GUY I COULD SEE WHO WAS WAITING PATIENTLY AND I TWIGGED THERE WAS SOMETHING WRONG. HE WASN'T BUYING ANYTHING, AND HE LOOKED BOTH TROUBLED AND RESOLUTE. AFTER THE CROWD HAD CLEARED AWAY, HE ASKED IF HE MIGHT SPEAK WITH ME, AND I IMMEDIATELY HAD A PREMONITION IT WAS GOING TO BE ABOUT THE SONG 'AUSTRALIAN FLAG BIKINI'. WE'D CLOSED THE SHOW WITH IT TO A GREAT RESPONSE THAT NIGHT, BUT I WAS BECOMING AWARE OF THE SONG'S POTENTIAL TO RAISE THE IRE OF SOME PEOPLE

He began by letting me know he was a professional soldier and had recently spent time in Afghanistan. The Weddings used to get a fair bit of support from the armed services, and I can remember getting more than one letter from the Gulf War, so I wasn't surprised to be speaking to someone from an area of society so removed from my own.

The reasons people might choose to like a piece of art — a song, a band, a film, a book, are totally personal and often unpredictable. The lyrics, the beat, the people who introduced them to the performer or what they were doing at the time can have a massive effect on why someone does or doesn't like you as an artist. Having said that, I've never been one hundred percent comfortable with those who see my music and writing solely as some sort of patriotic exercise. I suppose it has to do with singing in a broader Australian accent than a lot of others and the use of colloquialism that lends our music to these ideals. I'm just really wary of jingoism generally, and don't like anyone assuming these songs were written for that purpose.

So we talked about Afghanistan for a while and about army life in general, and then he finally began to make his point: that he had an objection to the song and felt it was disrespectful to the flag, and to patriots in general. He was in no way belligerent — just troubled by what he saw as someone making light of something he felt was serious and sacred. I countered by asking if taking a cheap reproduction of the flag and draping it over a woman's body in a lewd and provocative way was insulting and demeaning to it in the first place. And wasn't the whole railroading of the Anzac myth into sport somehow a corporate construct of the commercial television networks?

When I hear the various sporting (mainly AFL) coaches invoking the Anzac spirit on the field I'm reminded of World War II veteran and Test cricketer Keith Miller's comment regarding pressure on the field: 'Pressure is a Messerschmitt up your arse; playing cricket is not.' I think even if you were someone with a belief in the flag and the so-called national ethos, surely you could still admit that it's been subject to some pretty crass and exploitative usage in the past few decades.

The fact I come from a family with a pronounced history and association with the armed forces in both world wars has been well reflected in my writing to date. What I would really stress here is that my father, as a long-serving and decorated member of the Australian Navy, was never a flag-waving zealot. If he was a patriot he was a gentle one and, I might add, a troubled one. As a nineteen-year-old he'd stood in the rubble of Hiroshima a week after the blast and was left wondering until the end of his days what it was all about. Years later he watched a documentary that argued the war was pretty well won by the time the Americans chose to drop those bombs, and this perplexed and troubled him deeply. I can never remember him going to the RSL and I know he never tried to coerce me into marching with him on Anzac Day, as I'm hardly aware he ever marched himself.

And so, back to the after-show exchange at the Oakleigh RSL. I ended up having a really good in-depth conversation with the guy, and I think we both might have gotten something out of it. Although, as it goes in these situations, you don't really ever change anyone's mind. My discomfort at any overt display of jingoism remains — especially when it is aligned with my music.

The song was written after being confronted by various exhibitions of ugly Aussie behaviour over the years, in particular a pretty tough gig in the beer garden at the Australian Open tennis tournament a few years back, but more significantly after playing at the Gympie Muster. Here we witnessed an unpleasant stall selling awful racist 'Fuck Off We're Full' stickers, and Australian flag t-shirts and bikinis (all manufactured in China, as far as I could see).

Earlier this year on a trip to Bali, I couldn't believe the shops in Kuta selling the same appalling racist rubbish. Locals selling the same racist 'Aussie, Aussie, Aussie' slogans for the sake of the Australian dollars we've convinced them they so badly want.

'Australian Flag Bikini' was recorded with an extended line-up of the Roving Commission for the *Christmas Day at Spencer Street* album. That's Dave Folley on drums, Zane Lindt on bass, Wally on accordion, John Bedggood on violin and Nick O'Mara on mandolin.

Preceding page left: Mick on the Anzac chair at the Caravan Club, Oakleigh RSL. Melbourne, 2013. Photo: Mark Hopper

Preceding page right: Mick in North Western Australia a few days after the last WPA show at Belvoir Amphitheatre, 1998

Opposite: Roving Commission at Flinders Street Station. From left: Mick, Zane Lindt, John Beddgood, Dave Folley, Wally, Nick O'Mara and Gus Agars. Melbourne, 2014. Photo: Mark Hopper

AUSTRALIAN FLAG BIKINI
(AFB)

M. THOMAS

MUSHROOM MUSIC

Note: the chord I write as Ao7 is a diminished 7th chord, and to the best of my knowledge the notes F# C D# A are what constitutes this.

(verse)

| E / / / | E / / / | F#m / Ao7 / | E / / / |

I'm not sure what I think of you in your Australian Flag Bikini

| E / / / | E / / / | F#m / Ao7 / | E / / / |

I'm not sure what to make of you in your Australian Flag Bikini

| Bm / / / | Bm / / / | A / / / | A / / / |

A patriotic girl I know You're looking good and even though it was

| A / / / | Am / / / | F#m / Ao7 / | E / / / |

sown in a sweatshop in Guangzhou your Australian Flag Bikini

AUSTRALIAN FLAG BIKINI
(AFB)

I'm not sure just what's the deal with your Australian Flag Bikini
I'm not quite sure what I should feel for your Australian Flag Bikini
I should be turned on I guess
But the Union Jack on your right breast
Just reminds me that we lost the test
In your Australian Flag Bikini

So your father let you out like that in your Australian Flag Bikini
And did your poor old mum say Slip slop slap to your Australian Flag Bikini
I guess they thought you looked a sport
In the flag for which your granddad fought
And the Hyundai which their money bought
In your Australian Flag Bikini

Well I'm not sure I'd talk so loud in your Australian Flag Bikini
I'm not quite sure I'd be so proud in your Australian Flag Bikini
Unless I am to understand
For those awaiting on remand
You've drawn a line in the Cronulla sand
In your Australian Flag Bikini
In your Australian Flag Bikini

So do you think I'm being just a touch unfair to your Australian Flag Bikini
As you shake back your long blonde hair in your Australian Flag Bikini
A patriotic girl it's true
You know half the lines to 'Hey True Blue' (but remember)
Melanoma's homegrown too
In your Australian Flag Bikini
In your Australian Flag Bikini
In your Australian Flag Bikini

Australian Flag, Australian Flag, Australian Flag Bikini

CHAPTER
- 31 -

FOR A SHORT TIME

A FEW YEARS BACK, PAUL GENONI WROTE TO ME SEEKING PERMISSION FOR HIS ARTICLE TO BE PUBLISHED. I THINK IT'S AS GOOD A WAY AS ANY TO FINISH THIS SELECTION OF STORIES THAT BEGAN WITH SONGS. IT'S A GREAT PIECE.

Grey skies over Melbourne: Grand Final Week 2012

First published in T. Dalziell and P. Genoni (eds), *Telling Stories: Australian Life and Literature, 1935–2012*. Clayton: Monash University Publishing, 2013: pp. 594–600.

This was never going to be an ordinary Melbourne week. After all this one has a name — Grand Final Week. The name refers of course to the deciding match of the Australian Football League (AFL) season. The Grand Final, traditionally played on the last Saturday in September, is the most well attended and widely broadcast climax to the seasons of the nation's various football codes. But it is much more than a single game of football. As the name suggests Grand Final Week is an extended celebration of the AFL code and its role as the winter heartbeat of Australia's most renowned sporting city. It is a week in which — usually — little else cuts through the Melbourne news cycle.

The story of Grand Final Week 2012 took shape as the two finalists, Melbourne's Hawthorn (Hawks) and the Sydney-based Swans, were decided by matches played on the Friday and Saturday of the previous weekend. Between the playing of these two Preliminary Finals, however, another event occurred that would dominate the news and push the Grand Final from the front pages in the AFL's showcase week. A woman disappeared from the streets of Melbourne.

This story has a second beginning. In late 1997, Melbourne-based folk-rock group Weddings, Parties, Anything released their final studio album, *River'esque*. The collection included 'For a Short Time', a song that became a regular addition to their live shows up until they played the final gig of their 'break up' tour in Perth in January 1999. 'For a Short Time' quickly became a fan favourite, a gentle and meditative sing-along usually played at the tail end of a boisterous night.

'For a Short Time' was written by the Weddings singer and songwriter, Mick Thomas. By the time the group disbanded Thomas had guided them through fifteen years, a number of line-up changes and seven albums, while struggling to 'make it' in the highly competitive world of Oz-rock. And although commercial success on the back of record sales was elusive, the Weddings developed a reputation as a formidable live band and built up a famously loyal following. The band regularly sold out pubs and clubs around the country, but they also remained an intrinsically Melbourne band, with Thomas's songs peppered by stories about the everyday life of the city, and in particularly its inner-city suburbs and communities. Such was the impact of the band on its Melbourne audience that their final shows in the city were the subject of both an *Australian Stories* program on ABC TV, and a one-man play, *A Party in Fitzroy*, by Victorian dramatist Ross Mueller.

The lyrics of 'For a Short Time' were somewhat elusive. For although the song clearly told the story of a brief yet fondly remembered encounter between the singer and a woman, the precise circumstances and the nature of the relationship were unclear. And while the song spoke of the woman being 'gone for good', it was not fully apparent if this referred to her having died or simply gone elsewhere.

> Tell me how long is a short time,
> is it longer than two hours,
>
> Or a bit less than a weekend,
> is it shorter than a year?
>
> Is it the time it takes to not complete
> your business with a person,
>
> With a friend you make in transit,
> to a daughter held so dear.

But these lack of specifics allowed the song to work as a generalised meditation on transitory meeting and parting, and as heard on *River'esque* — in the context of an album bringing the curtain down on the band's career — and performed on stages as the Weddings might their final trek across the country, 'For a Short Time' assumed an elegiac tone. The tale of transitory meeting and separation allowed the song to serve as a farewell of sorts, an acknowledgement of the need to make the most of the 'short time' the band and audience had together.

> Sometimes you can say more,
> in a drunken hour or so,
>
> Than some people get across,
> in a life of lying low,
>
> And sometimes you can feel more,
> for someone you've barely kissed,
>
> But you don't see it at the time,
> and the moment that you've missed.

Preceding page left: Mick Thomas and the Roving Commission at the Mollongghip Hall. From Left: Mick, Sal Kimber, Julien Chick. Mollongghip, 2013

Preceding page right: WPA. From left: Jen Anderson, Michael Barclay, Mick, Paul Thomas, Stephen O'Prey and 'Squeezebox' Wally

Opposite: From a march in response to the tragic death of Jill Meagher. Melbourne, 2012

After the demise of the Weddings the six band members went their various ways, either surfacing in other bands or returning to former lives. Thomas fronted a new band, The Sure Thing, with whom he continued to record and perform. Amongst the new repertoire he kept 'For a Short Time' as part of his live sets, where it typically retained its position as the closing song. In performance, Thomas began to precede the song by telling a poignant, sorrowful, but also humorous story of how the song came to be written. He recounted how the Weddings had a brief encounter with a young Australian female fan after a gig in Canada, and how she'd hung out with them for a time drinking and playing pub games as they wound down after the show. As they decided to kick on into the later night she was invited to join them for an extended party — an invitation she declined. They parted with vague suggestions of catching up later back in Australia.

Thomas's story — told over an occasionally strummed guitar teasing at the edge of the song's melody — recounted how this brief meeting had its unexpected sequel some time later at a gig in Australia, where he was handed a note from the audience with a woman's name and the notation, 'R. I. P.' Thomas shared the note with the band as they tried to discover who the girl was, and while at first they couldn't recall her, eventually the connection was made, and memories of that Canadian night and the now deceased young woman came flooding back. Telling this story was presumably a strategy used by Thomas to have his audience share the full meaning of his lyric, to have them understand his song and how the potential and fragility of this fleeting encounter became significant only in retrospect.

It was a football match that led Thomas to resurrect Weddings, Parties, Anything in June 2005, when the band played at the annual Community Cup charity match. Thomas declared that the reunion wasn't permanent and that the band would simply come together for occasional shows. Several short tours followed, but generally performances remained few and far between. One regular date the band has established in recent years is a one-off Melbourne show on the eve of the Grand Final. For long-time Melbourne fans the Weddings Grand Final eve gig is as much a part of Grand Final Week as the Brownlow Medal night, the Grand Final Parade, and the match itself.

And so it was that the members of Weddings, Parties, Anything gathered at the Palace Theatre, Bourke Street, on Friday night September 28, 2012. By any measure this annual gig came at the end of an extraordinary week in Melbourne. Jill Meagher, an Irish-Australian woman, had disappeared from the commercial and recreational precinct of Sydney Road, Brunswick, in the early hours of Saturday morning. The news of Meagher's disappearance was spread on social networking sites across the weekend as her husband, friends and family instantly realised that something was terribly wrong, and on Monday morning Melbourne awoke to hear that a young, attractive and vivacious woman was missing without explanation. The news was conveyed continually by the broadcasters and newsreaders of every radio and television station in the city, but most urgently by those at the ABC where Meagher worked. Their concern about the wellbeing of their colleague and friend was apparent in every word.

As the hours progressed, fear for Meagher's safety grew as details emerged of her night out with work colleagues; the missed opportunity to be escorted home; the late night phone call made in the minutes before she disappeared; her missing handbag located in a laneway; the removal by police of personal belongings from the apartment she shared with her husband. In those few days it was impossible to walk the streets of Melbourne; or sit in the city's cafés, bars or restaurants; or ride its trams, and not overhear, or be part of, conversations about Meagher's fate. And as the press competed for new angles the story increasingly became of Meagher herself — of her background, her schooling, her role at the ABC, her husband, and her family in Perth and Ireland. Coverage was fleshed out where possible with an ever-growing array of photos showing the missing woman at parties, on holiday, with family and friends, and at her wedding. Jill Meagher became seemingly 'known' by the whole city, and the personal element became as integral to the story as her last known movements. Many women in particular expressed the sudden vulnerability of realising they had walked those streets, been to those bars, and taken similar unescorted walks through the normally unthreatening suburb.

Meagher's story was also personal to Mick Thomas. Thomas had lived in Brunswick after moving to Melbourne from Geelong, and his affection for the suburb was expressed in the song 'Brunswick', written for the Weddings second album. The song was a fondly remembered portrayal of an inner-city working-class community, underpinned by a nostalgia for the people, sights and smells that had been the songwriter's introduction to big-city living.

Another, less benign portrait of Brunswick, and another crucial piece of Jill Meagher's story, emerged midweek in the form of some thirty seconds of CCTV footage taken on Sydney Road minutes before her disappearance. It showed Meagher being confronted by a man, his face largely obscured. The 'meaning' of the brief interaction was unclear, but it suggested something cajoling, perhaps intimidating on his part; hesitancy and very likely fear on hers. Suddenly the story of Meagher's disappearance became even more compellingly personal, as television relentlessly recycled the vision of these critical few seconds. The CCTV footage was clearly a breakthrough in the police investigation.

Within forty-eight hours a man had been charged with Meagher's rape and murder, and police announced shortly after that her body had been recovered from a makeshift grave in outer Melbourne. On Friday, just as the Grand Final parade featuring the Hawks and Swans wound through the city centre, the accused man appeared before the Melbourne Magistrate's Court. And as the day unfolded spontaneous memorials sprang up around the city — on Sydney Road where those final images were recorded; at the spot where her body was recovered; at the entry to the ABC offices; on the walls of inner-city laneways. Meagher's ABC colleague John Faine mourned his friend on air, noting the enormous impact of her death on the city, proclaiming that 'Jill's death must not come to define us. That is not what it is like to live in the Melbourne we know.'

It was into this atmosphere that Weddings, Parties, Anything stepped that evening to play their Grand Final gig — their only performance for the year. They were met at the Palace Theatre by a roomful of faithful fans and Friday night revellers. Doubtless many were hoping to indulge themselves and forget how tragically the previous Friday night had ended, and how relentlessly the week since had unfolded.

Appropriately, the band opened with 'The Swans Return', Thomas's good-natured account of the departure of AFL team South Melbourne to Sydney some thirty years before, and the loyalty of their hardcore fans waiting for their return to Melbourne. From there the lengthy set wound through highlights from the band's substantial back-catalogue, mixing Thomas's songs — many replete with footballing references ('Is there anywhere that you'd rather be than with me at the MCG?') — with well-established covers that fitted seamlessly with Thomas's own stories. So that his song of colonial excess 'A Tale They Won't Believe' was matched by the traditional 'Streets of Forbes'; the Depression era-based 'Hungry Years' was echoed in Tex Morton's 'Sergeant Small'; his version of the Australian pastoral in 'A Decent Cup of Coffee' faced its image in The Triffid's 'Wide Open Road'; and joyful tales of inner-city Melbourne in the form of 'Under the Clocks' and 'Roaring Days' met headlong with the Strange Tenants' sardonic 'Grey Skies Over Collingwood'.

After nearly three hours before a typically enthusiastic crowd, the band came to their final encore, and their last song of the night. Correctly, the crowd anticipated 'For a Short Time' as the closing number, but Thomas prepared them anyway. Dispensing with the by now familiar story behind the song, he spoke instead of Melbourne, of community and unity, of *this* night before the city's big day, coming as it did at the end of *this* week. Surveying the crowd and taking its measure he commented on the presence of rival fans standing side-by-side, wearing the colours of the Hawks and the Swans, adding that this capacity to come together despite difference was something to 'love about Melbourne'. He noted that since the Weddings had played at this venue on Grand Final eve twelve months previously 'we are missing a few people'. The band, he said, had lost three friends, before adding, without the need for detail, that Melbourne 'has lost more as a town'.

The crowd was stilled as Thomas led the band into 'For a Short Time', as they heard it remade from a story about a Canadian night, many years before, and an unknown woman, into a story from their own place and time, and a woman now known to every member of the audience. On the back of the familiar melody and lyrics and Thomas's own vocal the crowd found its voice, singing both the verses and the chorus, finding in the lyrics a story that had now grown to encompass their own recent experience of a life briefly glimpsed and so finally lost.

For a short time, she was standing there, and you saw her,

She saw you and you recall the colour of her hair.

For a long time, you never thought of her,

Then you heard she was gone for good,

You might have cried then if you could,

Would have looked foolish if you did,

Somewhere the tears are falling in your mind,

For a short time.

The final verse of 'For a Short Time' is something of an apocryphal lyric in the Weddings canon. It was not included in the recorded version of the song, and not always performed when played live. When sung it arrives as a final poignant coda added at a point where the song has seemingly reached its logical conclusion — a last wrenching confirmation of the nature of sudden, unexpected and final separation. On this occasion as the band arrived at the song's close Thomas reached for this final verse. As he did so the music fell away, at first seemingly slowed, and then silenced, by the weight of the crowd singing and whispering the familiar words. The band let their instruments fall and stepped forward to sing *a capella*, sharing the burden with their singer and the audience.

> Faces come and faces go,
>
> In the ragged life you lead,
>
> But you just file them all away,
>
> You recall them as you need,
>
> When a face just disappears,
>
> You report it as a crime,
>
> Against yourself, against the world,
>
> For a short time.

As the song reached its hushed conclusion some of the crowd cheered and clapped their appreciation, but many others turned away in silence, wiping tears from faces.

Thomas singing 'For a Short Time' in this way, at this time, could of course no more change the fate of Jill Meagher than singing 'The Swans Return' could alter the outcome of the Grand Final. But it did have the power to change how those present might understand that event; of the explanations that might be given to the inexplicable, and of the capacity for a community to draw heart and hope at a time that might otherwise have seemed heartless and hopeless.

The next day the MCG played host to 100,000 spectators as the Swans did indeed return — at least briefly — and took the AFL Premiership Cup back to Sydney after an epic Grand Final. Questioned after the game as to whether the loss was a tragedy for his team, losing coach Alastair Clarkson drew the curtain on his week by declaring that the Grand Final was merely part of the 'theatre of sport', and that Jill Meagher's death was an example of a 'true tragedy'. And on the day after that 30,000 people gathered on Sydney Road on the back of word-of-mouth and a social networking campaign, and walked together in a show of grief and despair, and in memory of a woman and a story that had shifted the heart of a city.

FOR A SHORT TIME

M. THOMAS — MUSHROOM MUSIC

*On Riveresque we play this one in D,
but it sounds better played in C using the capo on the 2nd fret.*

(intro)
| C / / / | C / / (B) | C / / / | C / (B) (G) |

(verse)
| C / / / | G / / / | Am / / / | F / G / |
Some - times you can say more in a drunken hour or

| C / / / | G / / / | Am / / / | F / G / |
so Than some people get across in a life of lying

| C / / / | G / / / | Am / / / | F / G / |
low And sometimes you can feel more for someone you've barely

| C / / / | G / / / | Am / / / | F / G / |
kissed But you don't see it at the time and the moment that you've

(chorus)
| C / / / | G / / / | Am / / / | F / G / |
missed For a short time she was standing there And

| C / / / | G / / / | Am / / / | F / G / |
you saw her and she saw you And you recall the colour of her

| C / / / | G / / / | Am / / / | F / G / |
hair For a long time you never thought of her Then

| C / / / | G / / / | Am / / / | F / / / |
you heard she was gone for good You might have cried then if you could

| G / / / | G / / / | F / / / | F / / / |
Would have looked foolish if you did somewhere the tears were falling in your

| G / / / | G / / / | F / G / | C (intro) |
Mind For a short time

FOR A SHORT TIME

(verse)
There's a photo of your gang on the night she hung about
And you're looking like a wag you've got your fat tongue poking out
But she is nowhere to be seen you won't spot her anywhere
It was her who took the picture you were looking straight at her

(chorus)

(verse)
Tell me how long is a short time is it longer than two hours?
Or a bit less than a weekend is it shorter than a year?
Is it the time it takes to not complete your business with a person?
With a friend you make in transit to a daughter held so dear?

(verse)
Faces come and faces go in the ragged life you lead
You just file them all away you recall them when you need
When a face just disappears you report it as a crime
Against yourself against the world for a short time

Mick Thomas and the Roving Commission at Stovepipe Studios. From left: Rowan Matthews (engineer), Mick, Matt Walker (producer), Dave Folley, 'Squeezebox' Wally and Michael Hubbard. Upwey, 2015. Photo: Mark Hopper

The Albums

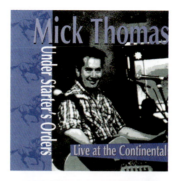
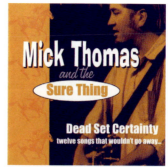

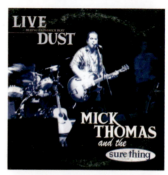

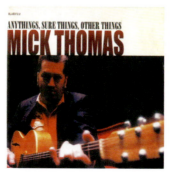
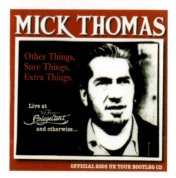

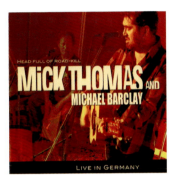 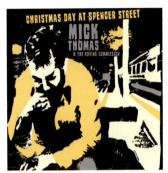

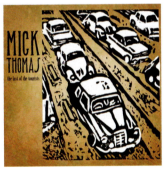 

All album cover art by Jen Huntley

ACKNOWLEDGEMENTS

Large thanks go to Jock Serong and Carolyn Logan, for constant positivity about this project.

To all the players post-weddings, parties, anything — the Sure Things and Roving Commissioners, who have shown so much patience with these songs and been part of these stories as they took place. In rough order of appearance:

Mark McCartney/Darren Hanlon/Rosie Westbrook/Ryan James/Michael Barclay/Craig Pilkington/Sandy Brady/Stuart Speed/Rory Boast/Al Barden/Anna Burley/Jeff Lang/Jen Anderson/Marcel Borrack/Phil McLeod/Mark 'Squeezebox' Wally/Zane Lindt/Julian Chick/Trent McKenzie/Gus Agars/Dave Folley/Cat Leahy/John Bedggood/Nick O'Mara/Michael Hubbard/Ayleen O'Hanlon

And to Jen Huntley, for art, for listening, for advice ... for everything, really.

THE AUTHOR

Mick Thomas was born in the Latrobe Valley and spent his childhood travelling Victoria with an itinerant SEC family. By his early twenties he was living in Melbourne playing in bands ultimately forming the Weddings, Parties Anything group which disbanded in 1998. He is currently defying gravity with Squeezebox Wally and the Roving Commission and when not lugging his sorry arse down the highway is a card carrying member of the Old Fathers of Northcote Society. Like most guitarists his age he is looking for a lighter amplifier.

Mick, Wally and the Sure Thing. Greendale, 2011. Photo: Mark Hopper

The companion album to this book, *These Are The Songs*, released by Liberatio Music, is available in record stores and from *mickthomas.com*